Acknowledgements

I have worked with a great many headteachers and teachers over the years whose comments, questions, philosophy and practice have significantly influenced my personal approach to both classroom teaching and encouraging colleagues to develop their practice.

In particular, I wish to thank:

- David Potter for his personal support over a great many years and for his willingness to share his considerable insight and extensive experience. His views have challenged, sharpened and helped shape my own and have added an invaluable dimension to this book

- Hull International Leadership Centre for their support and encouragement and for giving me the opportunity to trial much of the material in this book

- The headteachers of Langdon Park School in Tower Hamlets, Barnwell School in Hertfordshire, Dene Magna School in Gloucestershire, Cheshunt School in Hertfordshire and Richmond School in North Yorkshire, for agreeing to share their experiences and practice in the form of ideas and case studies, and to Chris Dunne, Carol Netscher, Jim Lamey, Richard Westergreen-Thorne, Paul Barnett, Mark Davies, Annette Knight, Tricia McCarthy and Maggie Kalnins for writing the case study material

- Nigel Cooke and John Brown for their faith and encouragement in the early days

- Gareth, Gerald and Phil for setting the standards for others to follow and Duncan, Trevor, Alex and Alan – a constant source of inspiration

- Rebecca Smith who never ceases to amaze me

- Dorothy Kelly for her help with the early manuscript, Lyn Johnson for tweaking the title and Gina Walker for her support and advice at the editing stage

- Rachel for her tolerance and unfailing good humour!

- Ben and Sam for making me play with them when I really should have been working.

I have tried hard to acknowledge the original sources of materials; please accept my apologies for any oversights.

Mike Hughes, May 2002

tweak to
TRANSFORM

improving teaching: a practical handbook for school leaders

Mike Hughes

with David Potter

Published by Network Educational Press
PO Box 635
Stafford
ST16 1BF
www.networkpress.co.uk

First published 2002
Reprinted 2005

ISBN 1 85539 140 6

Editor: Gina Walker
Design and layout: Neil Hawkins

Printed in Great Britain by
MPG Books Ltd, Bodmin, Cornwall

Contents

Management, by definition, is limited in its scope, horizons and possibilities. We are only now beginning to explore the potential of leadership in education.

Foreword

By Professor John West-Burnham

Over the past decade or so there has been a slow, at times almost imperceptible, change in education which is having the cumulative effect of challenging every orthodoxy of the past 100 years. The change centres on our understanding of the nature of the learning process and how that impacts on the role of the pupil, the work of the teacher, the nature of the school and the purpose of management and leadership. In each case, it is clear that historical, well-established (comfortable) patterns of working are increasingly untenable – in essence, the status quo is not an option.

Therefore, change must become the norm – which, in fact, it always has been. Children change as they learn; teachers have always been initiators of that change. Schools as organizations have proved remarkably resistant to change – it is bizarre that the most profound changes in society are increasingly taking place *in spite* of the organizations that should be the most supportive. Management, by definition, is limited in its scope, horizons and possibilities. We are only now beginning to explore the potential of leadership in education.

For all these reasons this book by Mike Hughes is very welcome. What he has done is provide an integrated model, an holistic view, which brings together the complexities of learning and leadership within the context of a real understanding of what change means. In many ways learning and leadership are symbiotic – both involve changing and being changed – both are about transforming and being transformed. However, this is not another exhortation to improve. Mike Hughes provides a reasoned and systematic approach to profound change by focusing on real and significant changes in practice and behaviour.

In this realistic, humane and practical study, Mike Hughes recognizes and respects the reality of life in schools while stressing the importance of a long-term perspective focused on the learning of every individual.

The quality of learning is directly related to the quality of teaching, which is in turn a function of the quality of leadership. Every page of this book offers insights, guidance and challenge – both in its content and presentation the book models an approach rooted in learning.

Books can only ever offer information; it is for the reader to understand and create knowledge and then to apply and extend it. *Tweak to Transform* offers a powerful resource to support reflection, create understanding and inform practice.

John West-Burnham
Professor of Educational Leadership
University of Hull

Schools are constantly being challenged to raise standards and improve results.

Where will *your* next '5%' come from?

- From doing things the same way?

- From doing things dramatically differently?

- From making small but significant adjustments to existing good practice?

Section One
Introduction

The purpose of this book

This book is about what headteachers and school leaders can do to manage the change process required to improve the quality of teaching in a school.

It does not claim to be the 'right answer' – it is simply a collection of thoughts, prompts, strategies and models, which are based upon extensive experience in a wide range of schools. It acknowledges that there is no single recipe for improving teaching in a school – there are, however, some basic ingredients.

Tweak to transform

As anyone who has ever tried will surely testify, encouraging teachers to try out new ideas in the classroom and to develop their practice is far from easy. Yet few would disagree that improving the quality of teaching in a school lies at the heart of genuine and sustainable school improvement. It presents headteachers and senior school leaders with a considerable challenge.

This book is underpinned by the belief that few people, in any walk of life, make *dramatic* changes to the way in which they operate – very rarely are practices suddenly *transformed*. Teaching is no different. If teachers are going to make changes, they are more likely to make small changes – *tweaks* – to their current practice. Sufficient teachers making sufficient tweaks, as part of a managed process, can add up to a significant improvement in the quality of teaching in a school.

Tweaking involves making *small but significant adjustments* to existing practice. As such it is a reassuring and realistic way of approaching change. There are a variety of reasons why teachers are more likely to tweak than transform – that is, make small adjustments rather than large-scale alterations to their classroom practice.

● Many teachers are *unwilling* to make dramatic changes quickly. Most people are wary of change – the bigger the change, the greater the reticence.

● Many teachers *do not need* to make dramatic improvements. Most teachers are doing a good job with most of the students, most of the time and the proportion of lessons that Ofsted now judge to be 'good' or better is higher than ever before. The capacity for large-scale improvements therefore simply isn't there.

● Some teachers are *unable* to make dramatic improvements. There may be teachers who are struggling in the classroom and require some significant improvements to their practice – but these people are unlikely to have the ability to make the changes in one go. If it were that simple, they would have done it long ago.

It is not possible to identify one single recipe for improving the quality of teaching.

It is, however, possible to identify some basic ingredients.

An emphasis on tweaking does not imply a belief that teaching cannot be significantly improved. It can. Indeed, there are many examples of how individual teachers or schools have substantially improved their practice. This emphasis simply acknowledges that significant improvement is usually the result of a series of smaller steps.

In isolation, the steps may seem almost inconsequential, but together they add up to something much more significant. Tweaking is a central feature of this book and is discussed in detail on pages 43–46.

Principles

This book is underpinned by the following eight core principles.

1   **The quality of teaching is the key to levels of achievement within a school. Not surprisingly, there is an emphasis on teaching and learning in successful and improving schools.**

2   **Improving the quality of teaching and learning is therefore the key to genuine and sustainable school improvement.**

3   **Change involves leaving the 'comfort zone'. Understandably, most people are wary – even scared – of change.**

4   **It is the responsibility of the headteacher and the senior leadership team to initiate, drive and manage improvements in classroom practice.**

5   **All schools operate in a unique context. There is therefore no single correct way to develop the quality of teaching in a school.**

6   **You cannot *make* people change.**

7   **We are therefore seeking to make it *more likely* that more people will leave their comfort zones and develop their practice.**

8   **_Tweaking_ – making small but significant adjustments – is a realistic and effective way of approaching changes in classroom practice.**

However, the book also acknowledges the following to be true.

- There is no single correct way to improve the quality of teaching – 'There is more than one way to skin a cat'. Strategies that are effective in one school do not always successfully transfer to another.

- Headteachers and senior leadership teams have considerable experience and expertise in this area. A wide range of strategies are currently being employed to improve the quality of teaching in schools.

- There are inherent weaknesses in generalizations. There are exceptions to every rule and, in reality, situations are rarely 'black or white'.

- Improving teaching and learning – indeed, change of any kind – is a complex business involving a large number of interrelated and interdependent factors. In the Sections that follow, these factors have been broken down and isolated simply for the purposes of clarity, precision and understanding.

'… teachers really do make a difference … our findings suggest that, taken together, teaching skills, professional characteristics and classroom climate will predict well over 30% of the variance in pupil progress …'

Hay McBer, *Research into Teacher Effectiveness* (2000)

This book is designed to:

● encourage headteachers and senior staff to reflect upon and evaluate the systems and strategies that they currently employ in order to improve the quality of teaching and learning in their school.

● offer food for thought – to induce the response, 'I never thought about it like that before'.

● present a range of models and concrete strategies that schools can adopt or adapt in their quest to raise standards of teaching and levels of achievement.

The book seeks to address three questions.

1 What do we know about change? (Section Two)

2 What do we know about learning? (Section Three)

3 What do we know about leading and managing the improvement process? (Sections Four, Five and Six)

Section Three, *What do we know about learning?*, is a summary of the material in *Closing the Learning Gap* and *Strategies for Closing the Learning Gap*, both published by Network Educational Press Ltd. It may therefore be helpful to read this book in conjunction with them. Details of all references and recommended reading can be found on page 260.

Background

'For the last twenty years, school effectiveness researchers have been edging closer to the discovery that the single most important ingredient of the school is the good teacher.'

Professor John MacBeath

Teaching makes the difference

High quality teaching is the key to improving levels of achievement in a school.

Schools play an important role, external structures such as local education authorities and education action zones make a contribution, but it is *teachers* who make the difference. Ask any parent!

Indeed, Professor David Reynolds suggests that teachers and what he refers to as the 'learning level' are *three to four times more powerful* than the 'school level'.

Ask any parents if they want a satisfactory education for their child and they will say:

'No – an excellent one.'

Variations within schools

A key difference between excellent and less effective schools is the *consistency* of teaching quality. Schools that are judged by Ofsted to be less effective still have excellent teachers, who are every bit as effective as their colleagues in more successful institutions. However, schools that are judged to be doing less well *also* have a trailing edge of lower quality classroom practice. Successful schools, on the other hand, have succeeded in ironing out these differences.

It is the influence of class teachers that explains why achievement varies – often significantly – *within* a school. Such variation is of far greater significance than variation *between* schools. The message is clear – consistency pays dividends.

Teaching and school improvement

Many schools have made significant advances in recent years. A range of measures – tightening procedures, establishing a culture of learning and achievement, the introduction of revision classes, individual mentoring schemes – have all contributed to 'ratcheting' up standards by a couple of notches. Inevitably, however, at some point the improvement curve begins to plateau. Further gains will be hard won.

From here on, continued improvement is dependent upon improving the quality of teaching that is taking place on a daily basis. It means that any attempt to raise standards must be focused firmly on the classroom. If it is teachers who make the difference, improving the quality of teaching must lie at the heart of genuine and sustainable school improvement.

Managing teaching quality

However, managing the quality of teaching has been consistently cited in recent reports by Her Majesty's Chief Inspector (HMCI) as being among the weakest aspects of school leadership and management. It is both ironic and hugely significant that the factor that makes the biggest single difference to raising levels of achievement – improving the quality of teaching – is the aspect of management that schools would appear to do least well.

This is not meant as a criticism – encouraging teachers to try out new ideas and develop their practice is far from easy. It does, however, suggest that reflecting on existing strategies and structures for managing teaching quality is a worthwhile exercise for all school leaders.

Developing teaching quality is notoriously difficult. If this is the bad news, the good news is that schools appear to be succeeding. Indeed, the same reports that highlight the relative weakness of school leaders' ability to manage teaching quality also acknowledge signs of improvement in this area. There is a growing belief that teaching comprises a set of skills that can and should be improved – not because teachers are poor or incompetent, but because even the best can get better.

When is 'satisfactory' unsatisfactory?

When the PANDA says so.

When satisfactory is unsatisfactory

In most schools, there are teachers who are consistently teaching excellent lessons and achieving outstanding results. They quite probably do so in a way that inspires and motivates their students. The only concern that headteachers have about these teachers is how to hang on to them!

There are then a handful of teachers whose teaching is unsatisfactory. Managing these teachers is time-consuming, difficult and often unpleasant. However, when performance falls below an acceptable level, there are at least management strategies and options available to headteachers and school leaders. In the first instance, of course, they are seeking to help such teachers to improve and raise their performance to a satisfactory level. They cannot *make* them do so, but for the individual the choice is stark – improve or face a formal capability procedure. Thankfully, despite rumours to the contrary, the numbers of teachers who fall into this category are low.

The staff who cause headteachers the most headaches, are those who teach 'satisfactory' lessons. Firstly, and at the risk of gross oversimplification, these are the lessons that are often delivered in a dull, dreary manner. Not surprisingly, students are frequently bored and occasionally disruptive. Secondly, 'satisfactory' teaching often produces 'satisfactory' results – that is, results that are steady, mediocre or 'OK'. However, at a school level, 'OK' results are no longer sufficient. Ask the PANDA!

Schools that achieve such unremarkable, 'run of the mill' results will probably not compare favourably with similar schools and run the risk of being identified as coasting, 'stuck in a rut' or lacking the capacity to improve from within. 'Satisfactory' at the classroom level does not necessarily lead to 'satisfactory' at the school level. Schools are being placed under increasing pressure to achieve at a level considerably higher than 'adequate' and this involves teaching lessons that rise above the mediocre.

As school leaders, we are not seeking miracles – just a 5 per cent or 10 per cent improvement in the quality of the teaching would lead to a *significant rise in results*. It is often the difference between an 'OK' year and an excellent one, and makes improving satisfactory lessons the key to school improvement.

> **Satisfactory teaching produces 'OK' results – but we are not in the 'OK' era, we are in the 'improvement' era ...**
>
> **... and improvement involves *change*!**

The comfort zone

People operate on a day-to-day basis in their 'comfort zone' (shaded area). It is not comfortable because it is easy but because it is familiar. On a good day, people go to the edge of their comfort zone (X). On a bad day, they retreat to the bottom (Y).

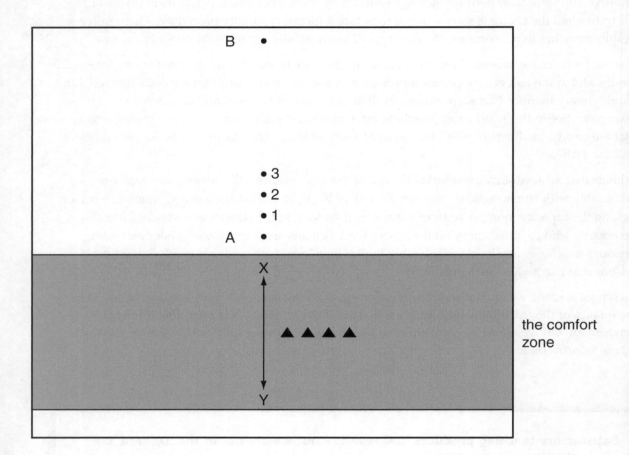

Change and the comfort zone

● People are more likely to go to A (tweak) than to B (transform).

● Large-scale changes (transformations) occur when we make a series of tweaks – that is, from 1 to 2 to 3, and so on.

● The triangles represent movement *along* the comfort zone – that is, new ideas that are not *that* different from current practice and are therefore not *that* threatening.

Section Two

What do we know about change?

> 'Change is not made without inconvenience, even from worse to better.'

Richard Hooker

This Section covers the following key points.

- Change involves leaving the 'comfort zone'.
- You cannot make people change – but you can create conditions conducive to change.
- Change is a managed process.
- Barriers to change must be overcome.
- People are more likely to make small changes than large ones.

Leaving the comfort zone

Change can be a daunting and, for many people, even scary prospect. Change, by definition, involves doing something differently and venturing away from the safety of the familiar. For some, it is an exciting – even exhilarating – proposition, but for many people it is a step that is only taken with great reluctance.

People generally operate on a day-to-day basis within their 'comfort zone'. Teachers are no exception. The comfort zone is a friendly and familiar place; it poses few threats. The person has been there and survived – and knows what to expect. This familiarity is reassuring and comforting and, understandably, acts as a magnet drawing people back to the place and position where they feel safe and in control.

Even when people recognize the need to change, they rarely do so, for the comfort zone is a hard place to leave. It's a bit like leaving your warm, snugly duvet on a frosty January morning – you know that you should be getting up but the prospect of it simply isn't that appealing.

Redefining the comfort zone

Leaving the comfort zone is just the first step. Improvement involves changing practice on a daily basis and establishing a new norm. This will only happen when the early experiences of doing

From unconscious incompetence to unconscious competence

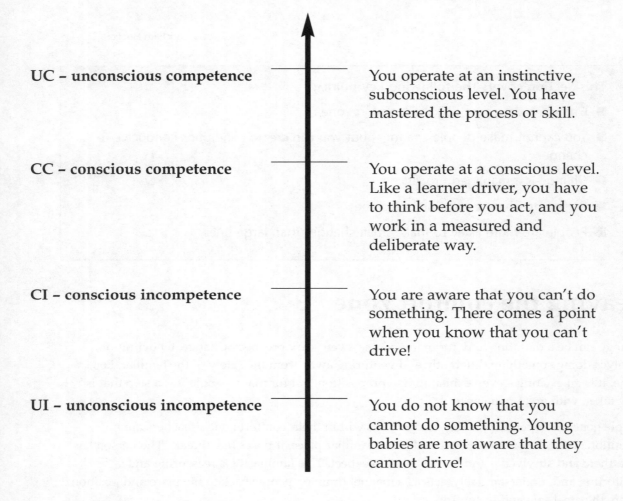

UC – unconscious competence

You operate at an instinctive, subconscious level. You have mastered the process or skill.

CC – conscious competence

You operate at a conscious level. Like a learner driver, you have to think before you act, and you work in a measured and deliberate way.

CI – conscious incompetence

You are aware that you can't do something. There comes a point when you know that you can't drive!

UI – unconscious incompetence

You do not know that you cannot do something. Young babies are not aware that they cannot drive!

Mastering a skill involves moving from a position of unconscious incompetence to unconscious competence. Breaking a habit demands conscious action. Change therefore involves moving from unconscious competence back to a state of conscious competence and even conscious incompetence.

something differently are positive – sufficiently positive to persuade you to try something again or, better still, to redefine your comfort zone.

Consider the use of ICT in the classroom. How many of us put off adopting an ICT dimension in our teaching even when we had accepted that we should? We had a range of perfectly good reasons for not doing so – reliable and staunch allies in our resistance to change – such as difficulties in booking the ICT facilities or inappropriate subject-specific software. Whatever the reasons we cited, and some had at least a degree of validity, they masked the fundamental lack of confidence that was at the root of our reluctance to change.

Perhaps, having finally surrendered to the endless nagging of a well-meaning ICT co-ordinator, we did eventually take a deep breath and venture falteringly into the brave new world of information and communications technology. Within minutes, our worst fears were confirmed as someone pressed the wrong button and turned the screen blank, the printer refused to co-operate and half the class discovered that the little ball in the mouse had been stolen.

Nightmares like this send us scurrying for cover, deep in the comfort zone, and the chances of our venturing out again, at least for some considerable time, are greatly reduced. Leaving the comfort zone is one thing, redefining it is something infinitely more challenging.

From unconscious incompetence to unconscious competence

When we have operated in a certain manner for a period of time, our actions become habitual and are largely driven at a subconscious level. Take, for example, driving a car. Experienced drivers just get in and drive with little conscious thought. They have negotiated a roundabout countless times before and their instinct will enable them to do so again, without the need to stop and think through their strategy. This is in sharp contrast to the conscious thought process and measured, deliberate action that occurs when a learner driver approaches such an obstacle.

Mastering a skill or a process involves moving through a series of phases, from unconscious incompetence, to unconscious competence (see opposite). When we have plied our trade for a number of years, habit and instinct replace conscious thought and we are able to operate at a mainly subconscious level. Breaking a habit and making a significant change involves a visit to the realms of conscious competence and even conscious incompetence – few go there with relish.

Breaking the habit

Even when people want to change, even when they are desperate to change, they often don't. How many fitness campaigns last less than a week? How many times have the best of intentions at the beginning of the new school year – the teacher's equivalent of a new year resolution – fallen by the wayside within a matter of days?

When people have operated in a certain manner for a period of time, they operate not only at a subconscious level, but also out of habit. Change involves breaking a habit, or, more accurately, creating a new one. This takes time and repetition – many experts would suggest that something needs to be done at least 20 to 25 times before it begins to become 'second nature'. Even when teachers want to change and try out something different in the classroom, unless they stick at it for a significant period of time, it is all too easy for them to slip back into their old ways – their habit – particularly when they are tired, stressed or in a rush.

I'm not in the habit of breaking habits.

Take the science department that had collectively agreed they should be spending more time at the end of their lessons summarizing and reviewing the work (see Section Three, *What do we know about learning?*). Every member of the team both recognized the importance of such practice and acknowledged that they frequently ran out of time as the lesson reached its conclusion and therefore simply omitted any form of meaningful plenary. There was a genuine commitment to change.

Six weeks later, however, nothing had changed. Every member of the team confessed that, despite their best intentions, they were still running out of time and forgetting to summarize at the end. Old habits die hard! Realising that good intentions alone would not break the habit, the science teachers asked the lab technician to visit each lab in turn and unobtrusively hold up ten fingers to remind them that there were only ten minutes of the lesson left. (They decided against a two-minute reminder!) Whatever they were doing, they would stop and review the work that had been covered. Gradually the lab technician began to notice that as she entered the lab towards the end of the lesson, more teachers on more occasions had already embarked on the review. A new habit was being created.

Conditions conducive to change

People are more likely to change when:

● they want to – change therefore involves what, how *and* why

● they feel it is safe to take a risk – change therefore requires a safe and supportive environment.

Change involves what, how and why

People are more likely to change when they want to, or at least accept the need for change. It means that, in addition to being clear about what they are going to change and how they are going to bring about that change, they have to accept why there is a need to do things differently.

In recent years, teachers have become accustomed to being told what to change. For example, the national strategies in literacy and numeracy, and other initiatives, have given teachers clear guidelines on how to teach. There is a growing view that teachers should be made aware of techniques and strategies that enable students to learn effectively and achieve high standards, and encouraged or even compelled to use them. When these directives and strategies are underpinned by extensive research, rather than driven by whim and myth, those who propound this case have a persuasive argument.

Whatever your personal views on the desirability of such a policy, it is important to recognize the world as teachers see it. In recent years teachers have increasingly been guided, even told, both *what* to teach and *how* to teach it. It is a trend that seems likely to continue in the foreseeable future.

The fact that schools do not control external or individual factors means that they must take every opportunity to create a safe and supportive professional environment in which teachers feel able and even encouraged to develop their practice.

Some teachers will, of course, accept the desirability of the changes being introduced – either immediately or eventually. Some will adopt new approaches and follow guidelines purely because they have been told to do so. Some, however, won't, and some of those that do – if they fail to see a valid reason for the change – will only do so with great reluctance. When this happens, there is a real danger that changes will be largely cosmetic and relatively ineffective.

Genuine, committed, sustained change is largely dependent upon individuals accepting the *need* for change, and this is more likely when they have been fully involved in the change process. When this role has been denied them at a national level – and this is largely outside of our control – it is arguably even more important to take every opportunity to allow teachers a creative role when working at school level.

The context for change

Leaving the comfort zone involves taking a risk. Change means 'different' and the inevitable consequence of 'different' is that things will get better or they will get worse. By definition, they will not stay the same. Understandably, therefore, people are more likely to venture from the comfort zone in a safe and supportive environment, when the inherent risk of change is reduced and the consequences of 'failure' are minimized.

Change does not take place in a vacuum – the context for change has a significant bearing upon an individual's attitude towards leaving the comfort zone. This context is created by a combination of:

- **external factors** – government policy, national strategies, and so on

- **internal factors** – the climate of the institution, how national strategies are interpreted and implemented, and so on

- **individual factors** – a combination of personal issues (for example, health and family matters) and professional issues (for example, stage of career and length of time in a school).

Schools and headteachers do not control either the external or individual factors. Indeed, there are many who would argue that external factors – league tables, a generally increasing accountability culture, an overcrowded curriculum and years of perceived criticism from politicians and press alike – hardly create a context conducive to risk-taking and development.

This feeling of pressure and unease is exacerbated when teachers hear talk of '*transforming* teaching and learning', '*revolutionizing* approaches to teaching' and '*radical* plans for Key Stage 3'. For most people interpret words such as 'transforming', 'revolutionizing' and 'radical' as meaning something significantly different – in other words, something a long way out of their comfort zone. And, as a general rule of thumb, the further out of the comfort zone you ask someone to travel, the less likely it is that they will say 'yes'.

The fact that so many factors that influence teachers' attitude towards change lie *outside* of a school's direct control makes it even more important that the school takes every opportunity to create an *internal* climate in which teachers feel able or even encouraged to develop their practice.

Motivators and demotivators

Factors leading to satisfaction (motivators)
- achievement
- recognition
- the work itself
- advancement
- responsibility

Factors leading to dissatisfaction (demotivators)
- externally imposed policy and administration
- supervision (for accountability purposes)
- relationship with supervisor
- work conditions

Factors having a largely neutral effect on motivation
- salary
- personal life
- status
- security

From F. Herzberg, *The Motivation to Work* (1959)

Note

The motivators are *different* from the demotivators –
not just opposite ends of the same continuum.

Change and performance management

One of the most significant external factors that affect attitudes to change within schools has been the introduction in the year 2000 of performance management for all teachers. Schools do not have a choice – they have to have a performance management policy. However, they do have a degree of choice over the way in which they interpret the requirements and implement the scheme. It is not the framework that varies so much between schools but the emphasis.

Work on motivation by many researchers, notably Herzberg (page 26, opposite), has shown that people at work, whatever their seniority or the type of work they are in, tend to be motivated by the same things:

- **achievement** – a sense that you are getting worthwhile things done and achieving success

- **recognition** – those you work with and for acknowledge the quality of your work and effort

- **the work itself** – you have job satisfaction; it is a job worth doing

- **advancement** – you are 'getting on', in terms of career development and/or the proficiency with which you do your job.

It is immediately apparent that performance management has the potential to press all of these motivator 'buttons'. The system focuses upon:

- discussion between you and your manager on key points for improving your teaching 'craft' (the work itself)

- acknowledging the strengths of your work; other colleagues are invited to learn from you (recognition)

- reviewing and acknowledging the progress you have made in the year (achievement)

- setting new, progressive goals (advancement).

However, Herzberg also identified a number of aspects of work that tend to *demotivate* people. These are the aspects of a job that don't make people happy when they are right, but do make people unhappy when they are wrong.

Such demotivators include things like 'supervision' – the sense of being monitored and overlooked in your work, with a clear implication that the purpose is to find fault – and, especially, 'company policy and administration'. This will be familiar to all teachers: another rule, form or piece of admin that takes you away from the classroom and the students.

There is a danger, therefore, that with a different emphasis – or at least perceived emphasis – performance management systems can just as easily press these demotivator buttons. Classroom observation – rather than being perceived as you and your team leader identifying your strengths, using them to help others in the team, and agreeing what you could do better – becomes snooping and fault finding. The whole system – instead of being seen as a way to celebrate individual and collective strengths with an emphasis on moving forward and developing – becomes another demotivating accountability exercise.

'The real problem is that perception is all that there is. There is no reality as such. There is only perceived reality.'

Tom Peters and Nancy Austin, *A Passion for Excellence (1985)*

Change and school climate

The climate or atmosphere of any institution is an important factor when an employee is deciding – even at a subconscious level – whether it is safe to take a risk and try something different. It would be foolish to underestimate the significance of climate simply because of the nebulous, abstract nature of the concept. It may be intangible, but it pervades thoughts, attitudes and decisions and is likely to be a highly influential factor as an individual decides whether to leave the comfort zone or not.

There are parallels here with the classroom. Just as the prevailing atmosphere of the classroom – a highly influential factor on the extent to which children will be prepared to take risks in their learning – is largely created by the teacher, so the atmosphere of the school is largely determined, or at least heavily influenced, by the headteacher.

Perception is everything

We are dealing here with perception – the feeling that we get as we walk into an institution. As headteachers, we may be striving to create a risk-free, supportive environment. We may even believe that we have succeeded. However, if the majority of staff do not share that view – if they 'feel' differently – we have a barrier to change that may prove to be insurmountable.

Perceptions are powerful and persuasive. They are often founded less on fact and more on the interpretation of small, subtle messages and almost intangible factors. Perceptions are also highly susceptible to peer influence; the view of a highly vocal, influential minority quickly spreads and, like a contagious disease, infects increasing numbers until it becomes the 'party line' and the 'staff view'.

Success in encouraging teachers to leave their comfort zone and develop their practice is largely dependent upon how they *perceive* performance management and other related attempts at improving the quality of teaching. Are they perceived as professional development tools or as yet more accountability exercises?

In your school, do you think risk-taking is:

- **frowned upon**
- **tolerated**
- **encouraged?**

How would the rest of the staff respond to this question?

If teachers believe that risk-taking is frowned upon or merely tolerated, they will be significantly less likely to take a perceived risk.

The most effective leaders seem to have erected a sheet of polaroid across the school gate: all the confusing, paradoxical and frustrating initiatives hitting the school, as they pass through the polaroid, emerge as parallel lines, harmonious with *our* plans and processes.

Change is a managed process

Change rarely happens by chance. The vast majority of people require a catalyst of some sort to prise them from the comfort zone. In the context of the school, this catalyst is often the headteacher and senior leadership team.

How many teachers drove to school this morning thinking, 'I really must improve the quality of my questioning' or 'How can I make my plenary sessions more effective?' Some may have done – probably people who are already teaching excellent lessons – but certainly not all, and certainly not many of the teachers whose teaching is currently satisfactory but no more.

> **The systematic, school-wide improvement of the quality of teaching is a managed process and it is the responsibility of the headteacher and senior leadership team to initiate and drive it.**

Winning the middle ground

> 'Progress occurs when we take steps which increase the number of people affected.'
>
> Michael Fullan

Improving teaching and learning across a school involves improving the performance of individual teachers. However, although we are interested in the aggregate effect of the actions that we take as school leaders, it is important to remember that individuals are motivated, and therefore influenced, in different ways. (The need to target our actions at individuals is considered in Section Four, *Leading the improvement process.*)

In most schools there are enthusiastic teachers who approach new ideas with an open mind and are often prepared to try out new techniques in the classroom. In many cases, of course, these are the teachers who are already doing an excellent job in the classroom. At the other end of the spectrum, there is also often a hard-core group of cynics who will not budge, no matter what.

This leaves a group of teachers in the middle ground. Neither enthusiasts nor cynics, they are essentially pragmatists and when convinced that an idea will work, and be of benefit both to them and their students, they will often give it a go. In many schools, these teachers represent the key battleground, simply because they comprise a sizeable majority. Win them over and a project gathers momentum; fail to win them over …

'Balance isn't either/or; it's both.'

Stephen R. Covey

- How effectively do you support teachers?
- How effectively do you challenge teachers?

Support and challenge

> **'The evidence is that successful innovation requires both pressure and support.'**

David Perkins

Headteachers support. Headteachers challenge. Some headteachers are naturally inclined to be supportive; others tend to adopt a more challenging approach to leadership and management. Successful, experienced headteachers, however, know that, whatever their natural tendencies, a *balance* is required and that, at times and in certain situations, the balance has to shift between the two. They also know that individuals on the staff are motivated by different factors; some will respond to encouragement and support, while others require a little more pressure and direct challenge before they will move. The point is that *both* are required, albeit in different measures on different occasions. Support alone will not bring about substantial school-wide change, nor will challenge on its own.

Often support comes first. Most schools have some enthusiastic teachers who will go away and try things after an INSET day. With these teachers, little or no management is required; enthusiasm alone will change the status quo. With encouragement and gentle cajoling, other teachers – broadly supportive of new ideas but a little reticent – can be persuaded to develop their practice, and gradually an initiative gathers momentum.

However, there will inevitably come a time when progress grinds to a halt and support will no longer be sufficient to spread new practice across the school. Further progress, and often the difference between an innovation taking root or wilting, is then dependent upon challenge and pressure. This is often the critical point. Winning over the enthusiastic teachers is relatively easy; the challenge, however, is to turn pilots into policy and policy into practice.

This means winning over the majority of the staff, although not necessarily all. Every school is different; some are blessed with more than their fair share of enthusiasts, while some have a greater number of cynics. For most schools, particularly medium-sized and large ones, the extent to which an initiative is adopted often depends upon convincing a 'critical mass' of staff and this in turn depends upon the extent to which headteachers and senior leaders are prepared to confront, challenge and ultimately win over the reluctant teachers in the 'middle ground'. In many respects, these teachers are the 'key marginals' (page 177).

If challenge is a key factor in persuading reluctant staff to develop their practice, it is rarely effective in isolation. For while many people need to be challenged to make a change, they also need to be supported as they make it. We do not simply desire that teachers change; we also want those changes to be effective, enhance learning and raise attainment. This almost certainly means that support is at least available during the vulnerable transitional period when people are developing both confidence and expertise working in a new way. Having either persuaded or pushed Bambi onto the ice, we must now support him as he finds his feet – otherwise it will have been a wasted effort (page 193).

In your school, are performance management and related attempts to improve teaching quality perceived as:

- a professional development tool, or

- yet another accountability exercise?

Workload versus ownership

David Perkins, in *Smart Schools*, suggests that when we are creating a context that is conducive to change and large-scale innovation, two of the necessary conditions are that:

- the innovation should not escalate teacher workload

- the innovation should allow teachers a creative role.

Both are significant issues. Many teachers would claim, with justification, that their workload has substantially increased in recent years. Many would also claim, with equal justification, that their professionalism has been severely eroded in recent times – increasingly, teachers are being told what to teach and how to teach it. Many would argue that both of these trends have contributed to what is widely acknowledged as a general demise in the morale of the teaching profession during the last decade or so.

The need to allow teachers a creative role in the change process and the need to avoid creating additional burdens of work can seem to directly contradict one another. It is undoubtedly hard, almost impossible, to fully satisfy both requirements simultaneously. However, this potential tension must be addressed and both factors taken into account if our attempts at encouraging teachers to develop their practice are to stand any chance of success.

Two lines of thinking are worth considering as we seek to establish a compromise position and address this dilemma.

1   We are seeking to establish a *balance* between, on the one hand, not significantly adding to the burden of already overworked teachers, while on the other, allowing them to feel involved in the process. There are those who would suggest that busy teachers simply want to be told what to do, given the necessary resources and left alone to deliver the goods. Maybe there are some teachers who would respond positively to this scenario. However, there are also significant numbers of teachers who wouldn't. Many teachers do not like to be told not only *what* to teach, but also *how* to teach it. There are many who derive considerable professional satisfaction from an active involvement in the development of classroom strategies and the production of teaching materials. What they would welcome, of course, is some time to do it!

2   To a certain extent, we are once again dealing with perception. Teachers need to feel that they have a creative role in the process – a degree of *ownership* – if they are going to give something their full commitment. Two schools may actually involve staff in the decision-making process in largely the same way and to a similar degree. However, it may be that in one school they *feel* involved while in another they *feel* excluded. Whatever the reality, teachers have to *feel* involved and that they have a valued and creative involvement in the process, as befits a professional.

Barriers to change

Barrier to change	Insignificant	Of some significance	Highly significant
(1) There is a lack of time for teachers to plan and prepare learning activities and to integrate new ideas into schemes of work			
(2) Good practice is not effectively disseminated throughout the department and/or school			
(3) There is a lack of time for senior leaders to monitor teaching quality and initiate, drive and manage developments in classroom practice			
(4) Teachers fear that new ideas will increase the risk of poor behaviour in the classroom			
(5) Many teachers perceive that they are being asked to do something *significantly* different from current practice, that is, venture way out of their comfort zone			
(6) There is scepticism that new ideas and initiatives are not helpful/practical/effective			
(7) There are too many conflicting initiatives/priorities			
(8) Teachers are unsure precisely what they are being asked to do – they are unclear about the difference between a satisfactory lesson and a good one. They are unable to translate general principles outlined during INSET into classroom strategies			
(9) Developments are not initiated, driven and managed at subject level			
(10) Teachers (at least some) resent being told what to do and how to teach. They do not feel part of the process			

Change takes time

> 'The story of successful change is understandably complex.'
>
> David Perkins

Few would dispute the assertion that change is a complex process. A multitude of factors – personalities, timing, chance events – all impact upon planned and desired changes. Not surprisingly, therefore, successful change takes time. Rarely are there quick-fix solutions. Nor is there a single recipe for successful change management.

This is not groundbreaking news. On the contrary, it is widely accepted that any attempt to change too much too quickly will almost certainly be doomed to failure. And yet the pressure to change and improve quickly continues to grow. We are in the 'instant age'; be it learning a language, losing weight or improving a school, there is an increasing desire to *do it quickly*. Understandably, there are times when this pressure becomes irresistible and we fall headlong into the trap of pushing the pace of change too quickly. It is equally understandable that when developments do not occur rapidly the apparent lack of success at bringing about change causes despondency and even dejection.

Often school leaders become frustrated at the pace of change. Improvements are being made but not as quickly as we would like. At these times, there is an understandable tendency to look forward and focus on the things that we have not yet done. It is important, of course, to keep the vision – but it is equally important to keep things in perspective. Change is a rocky road to travel; it is hard, it is complex and, above all, it takes time. Far from being surprised when we meet difficulties and barriers, we should *expect* obstacles and plan for them. Sometimes, we have to take a step backwards before we can take two steps forwards.

Even though we know this, it is all too easy to forget, and we would not be human if our resolve, enthusiasm and optimism were not tested from time to time. On these occasions it is important, not least for our own sanity, to reassure and remind ourselves of the progress that we have made. We should glance backwards on occasions and remind ourselves where we have come from.

Barriers to change

What stops, or at least hinders, teachers in your school from developing their practice as much or as quickly as you would like? What are the biggest barriers to change in your institution? Some of the factors that prevent, or at least hinder, change and improvements to classroom practice may well apply to teachers irrespective of context; some may be unique to your institution.

The exercise on the opposite page can be a useful starting point to both aid reflection and stimulate discussion about what, if anything, is holding you back. Having identified the obstacles, you can then turn your attention to removing, reducing or avoiding them. At the very least, senior leaders must be mindful of the potential barriers to change, and people's likely responses to it, as we launch an initiative or construct any improvement programme.

Time alone is rarely the key barrier or the root cause of a person's resistance to change.

Time

One of the most frequently cited barriers to changing and developing classroom practice is a lack of time for teachers to reflect, plan and prepare. This is clearly linked to the number of priorities and initiatives in which schools and teachers are involved, all of which compete for precious working time.

However, while no one can dispute that time is an increasingly scarce and significant resource – a situation that is by no means exclusive to education – there is an old adage: *'If you want something done, ask a busy person'*. As with many such pearls of wisdom, it is firmly grounded in reality. Consider the following.

- There are teachers who approach training with an open mind and enthusiastically embrace new approaches. They are busy too.

- Why are some schools more successful than others in managing and improving the quality of teaching and learning? They too suffer from 'initiative overload'.

- Think of a teacher who teaches satisfactory rather than inspirational lessons. Provide him or her with an hour a week to be used exclusively to reflect, plan and prepare. Do you believe that this strategy alone will significantly improve the quality of that teacher's lessons? Do you believe that the teacher will now embrace all of those new ideas, which, up to now, he or she has rejected?

- Teachers don't get enough time to reflect, plan and prepare. How much time would be enough?

Time is clearly an issue. It would be foolish to pretend otherwise. Additional time for teachers to prepare materials, and translate good ideas encountered during training into classroom tasks and activities, can often be the difference between good intentions and implementation. Particularly when it is part of a managed process and provided for a specific task with a measurable outcome, the provision of a little additional time can undoubtedly make a significant *direct* contribution to any drive to improve classroom practice. Teachers' disposition to change may also improve if they *feel* that they have been treated as professionals and been given the time to do a particular job – subtly altering teachers' perceptions of the change process in this way can therefore have an *indirect* but important benefit.

However, simply providing teachers with some extra time every week would be unlikely to make a significant difference to classroom practice. For time alone is rarely the key barrier or the root cause of a person's reluctance or resistance to change.

'Rather than pushing harder to overcome resistance to change, artful leaders discern the source of the resistance.'

Peter Senge

The root cause

There are people who don't have time. There are people who are sceptical, even cynical, about the value of some of the approaches being proposed. However, their overt cynicism can easily mask a fundamental lack of confidence that is often the root cause of an individual's reluctance to change.

We must not forget how scary change is for even the most seemingly confident individuals. For their confidence is often the product of familiarity. Once you have proved to yourself that you can do something, doing it again is unlikely to hold too many terrors for you. There are many teachers who have, over many years, developed practices and procedures that have enabled them to survive and even flourish in their professional environment. Understandably, they believe that they are held in high esteem by both the school and wider community. Even more significantly, they hold themselves in high esteem.

Change challenges their opinion of themselves. Their understandable fear is that they will not be successful, or at least not *as* successful, working in a different way. They believe that they are being put to the test and may be found wanting. Not surprisingly many lack the confidence to commit to such a process – this lack of confidence often manifests itself as scepticism and rejection.

For many teachers, the root cause of their lack of confidence and their reluctance to change is a fear of losing control. When teachers have to work hard to establish a working atmosphere and when they consider their hold on the class to be tenuous, their instinct tells them to tighten, not loosen, their grip. Consequently, they meet the challenge of behaviour management by playing safe, reducing risks and keeping firm control of proceedings in the classroom.

When they hear talk of 'engaging learners in an active process' and 'giving students increased responsibility for their learning', their belief, rightly or wrongly, is that they are being asked to teach in a way that increases the likelihood of poor behaviour. Not surprisingly, they are reluctant!

This is not to suggest that *all* cynicism is a derivative of insecurity. As professionals, teachers are understandably sceptical when they believe they are being asked to work in a way that is unhelpful, impractical or not conducive to high quality teaching and learning. The challenge for senior leaders is to recognize the difference between the two, and act accordingly. Do we need to persuade a teacher that there is merit in a strategy, or that he or she is capable of using it successfully? Making this distinction is no small task, for it is sometimes difficult to recognize and accept the source of our own scepticism and prejudices, never mind pinpoint the source of other people's negativity.

Yet only by identifying the root cause can we ensure that we are addressing the real barrier to change. And this is a key to successful change management. The context and therefore the specific challenges may vary from school to school, but the basic principle holds true; we must identify and then address the thing or things that are stopping people changing – otherwise things will stay the same.

We cannot make people change.

We are simply seeking to create conditions that will make it more likely that more teachers will leave the comfort zone and develop their practice.

Two central pillars

This book is based around two central pillars.

1   We can't make people change. We are therefore seeking to create the conditions that will make it more likely that more people on more occasions will be prepared to venture outside of the comfort zone.

2   Most people are more likely to make small adjustments than drastic, wholesale changes. 'Tweaking' is therefore a realistic way of approaching change.

We can't make people change

'If there is one cardinal rule in the human condition, it is that you cannot make people change.'

Michael Fullan

Just as there are teachers who desperately want to change but are struggling to break a habit, there are also teachers who, for various reasons, have significantly less enthusiasm for developing their practice! The bad news for headteachers and other senior staff who spend such a large part of their working life initiating, managing and responding to change is that we can't *make* people change. We can no more make a teacher adopt a certain practice than we can make a student sit quietly and pay attention or make a two year old go in the bath. Accept this and your stress level will come tumbling down!

If that is the bad news, the good news is that we can *influence* people. Indeed, we cannot *help* but influence them! Everything that we do and say will have an influence, consciously or inadvertently, positively or negatively. We can encourage, threaten, persuade or cajole; we can challenge and support. When we do so as a conscious strategy, we increase the likelihood that our efforts will have the desired effect.

Let us therefore redirect our professional energy and invest our time in influencing people. *We are simply seeking to create conditions that will make it more likely that more teachers will leave their comfort zone and develop their practice.* It is as simple, and as complex, as that!

Tweaking operates at two levels

Teacher or department:
How effective are you at helping children learn? Award yourself a mark out of ten for the quality of your teaching.

Senior leadership team:
How effective are you at persuading teachers to develop and improve? Award yourself a mark out of ten for how effective you are at *managing the improvement* of teaching in your school.

This is not an external judgement by a line manager or inspector.

Whatever mark *you* awarded yourself in either category, you will remain at that score until you find something to do differently. It doesn't have to be dramatically different – just a tweak.

This book is about helping school leaders to identify an aspect of their current management practice that they could develop in order to help teachers develop an aspect of their teaching.

In other words, what are *you* going to tweak to make it more likely that *they* will tweak?

Transform or tweak?

Tweaking is a more realistic approach to improving teaching and learning. It involves making *small but significant changes* rather than a complete overhaul. It is more likely to be successful for three reasons.

1   Teachers are more likely to be *prepared* to tweak – make small alterations to their approach – as opposed to making dramatic changes. Tweaking is more reassuring than transforming as it keeps teachers close to their current reality and only involves taking a small step out of the comfort zone. It may even amount to applying only 'a bit of polish' that doesn't require the teacher to do anything significantly different.

2   Teachers are more likely to be *able* to tweak.

●   Given the respective context, most teachers are doing a good – at least competent – job with the majority of the students on the majority of occasions. We are therefore seeking to improve from a high or 'highish' baseline. In other words, the capacity to improve is reduced. How would a golf coach improve Tiger Woods? By transforming his game or helping him to make some small but significant adjustments?

●   Even when we feel that a teacher has some considerable ground to make up before we would be satisfied with his or her performance in the classroom – someone who requires more than just a tweak – the chances of their being capable of making dramatic and significant changes in one go are extremely slim. If it were that easy to improve people, we would have done it long ago.

3   Tweaking can create a sense of purpose and generate a momentum that can become irresistible. When people have taken the first step out of the comfort zone and survived, they are more likely to take the next step and continue the development process. A journey of a hundred miles starts with a single step…

Two factors are fundamental to the notion of tweaking.

●   Tweaking demands a precision often lacking in improvement programmes. In order to make significant adjustments, we have to be very specific and accurately identify which bits we need to tweak. 'Improve teaching' and 'turn satisfactory lessons into good ones' are too vague. *Precise diagnosis* is a prerequisite for tweaking.

●   Having narrowed it down and identified the specific areas to work on, we must consider *how* to tweak it. In other words, what are the practical strategies – that will work within the constraints and context of the classroom – that teachers can introduce into their teaching to enable the tweak to be made? If we neglect this step and fail to generate the strategies and activities that teachers need to develop, even the most precise diagnosis will have little effect.

Tweaks can transform

Gareth didn't like Tuesdays. In particular, he didn't like first period on a Tuesday when, every week, he would have a test in history. He wasn't very good at tests – at least he didn't think he was – and every week as he walked into the history classroom, a little voice in his head reminded him, 'you're no good at tests – you hate this lesson'. Every week, in response to the little voice, the hairs on the back of his neck stood up, his heart beat a little bit faster and his palms began to sweat.

One day, suddenly, without warning, the tests stopped. Instead of a test in the last 15 minutes of the lesson, the teacher played noughts and crosses. This was more like it! This was a bit of fun! First the teacher asked the children to draw a giant noughts and crosses grid at the back of their books and number the boxes 1–9. Then she asked nine questions, the children writing down the answer in the appropriate box. If the question was answered correctly, a 'nought' was placed in the box, while a 'cross' denoted an incorrect attempt.

'Your challenge', explained the teacher, 'is to get a row, column or diagonal of noughts.'

'Bet you can't!' she added with a smile. 'Bet I can', thought Gareth and the game began.

'Yes!' he exclaimed to himself as a correct answer for number 7 completed a column of noughts. 'Told you I would', he whispered quietly. Now a column of noughts is still 3/9 – Gareth's average score in the weekly tests – but it certainly wasn't the way he was looking at it. He told his Mum about the game when he got home and even organized an impromptu competition between his sister and his Dad that evening.

The noughts and crosses game became a regular feature of Tuesday's history lesson and, judging by the clenched fists and the triumphant exclamations of success, Gareth was not the only student who enjoyed the challenge. Quickly, Gareth's attitude to Tuesdays changed. His confidence began to grow as he found himself getting more noughts than crosses. As the weeks went by, he found himself looking forward to history – his attitude towards the subject, and his belief in his own ability, completely transformed.

Summary

1 Widespread improvement rarely happens by chance. It is a managed process and it is the responsibility of the headteacher and school leaders to initiate, drive and manage it.

2 We can't make people change. We are therefore seeking to create the conditions that will make it more likely that more people on more occasions will be prepared to take a step out of the comfort zone.

3 This is more likely when we seek to make small but significant changes – tweaks – to classroom practice.

4 Any improvement programme is more likely to be more effective when we identify potential obstacles to progress and take steps to address them. We must also take into account what we know about people's reaction to change. It is therefore important to bear in mind that change:

▶ involves leaving the comfort zone – many people are wary, even scared of change

▶ requires people to break a habit – they therefore have to operate at a conscious level

▶ occurs in an institution when the number of people influenced by the new idea or approach increases

▶ requires both challenge and support

▶ is unlikely to be successful if it involves a significant increase in workload

▶ is more likely to be successful when teachers have a creative role in the process

▶ is a complex process – it takes time.

'There have been many attempts to define learning: many of them can leave a reader disappointed.'

C. Watkins, E. Carnell, C. Lodge and C. Whalley (2000)
in *Effective Learning (Research Matters series number 5), Institute of
Education, School Improvement Network, London*

Section Three

What do we know about learning?

This Section covers the following key points.

■ Learning involves making sense of information.

■ Learning is an active process.

■ State, style and structure are the keys to effective learning.

The last 12 years or so have seen an unprecedented interest in learning, much of it fuelled by dramatic advances in neuroscience and an increased understanding of the workings of the human brain. All around the globe, educators have been striving to take this increased knowledge about the brain into account when devising learning experiences.

There are people who claim that advances in the field of neuroscience, while fascinating, have told us little that we didn't already know about learning. Maybe this is true. However, whether discoveries about the workings of the brain have informed, challenged or simply validated traditional approaches to learning, there is no doubt that they have spawned an unparalleled interest in the subject.

This book does not promote a single, particular approach to learning. It does, however, suggest that it is important to take into account what we know about learning, when we are considering how to make teaching more effective.

The focus of this book is how school leaders manage the improvement of teaching. This Section is therefore intended as no more than a brief summary of the key issues discussed in *Closing the Learning Gap* and *Strategies for Closing the Learning Gap*. Further recommended reading is suggested on page 260.

What is learning?

Learning is our core business, with thousands of teachers sharing the same basic job description: 'My job is to help children learn'. Yet ask each of these teachers to define the word 'learning' and you will receive many different replies. Many of them will focus upon teaching rather than learning, many will focus upon transferring information rather than making sense of it, and many will focus upon knowledge and information rather than understanding.

'We would wish to stress the central importance of a school's developing a common and shared understanding of the word "learning" which is meaningful to that community and applicable to that particular context.'

Christopher Bowring-Carr and John West-Burnham

- Do all the teachers in your school have a shared understanding of the word 'learning'?

- Does it include reference to understanding?

This confusion does not help our cause, not least because the way in which we interpret the word 'learning' will have a significant influence on the way in which we teach. When the emphasis is on transferring rather than making sense of information it is all to easy for learners to be reduced to passive, sponge-like recipients of the teacher's wisdom.

This is in sharp contrast to a view of learning as an active process involving individuals making sense of new information and experiences. And that is precisely what learning is. If an agreed definition of 'learning' continues to prove elusive, there is a much broader consensus of the fundamental principles that underpin the learning process.

The key principles of learning

> 1   Learning involves making sense of information.
>
> 2   Learning involves building on existing understanding.
>
> 3   Learning takes place at a level just beyond current understanding.

Learning involves making sense of information and experiences

> 'Learning occurs when the penny drops, the light comes on and the learner exclaims, "Ah, I get it!"'

However you personally define the word, few would disagree that understanding lies at the heart of learning. Teachers may struggle for a scientific definition, but all would recognize the 'Ah, I get it!' moment when the penny drops or the light comes on. And this is learning. It is the moment that an individual makes personal sense of information that has come their way.

The 'Ah, I get it!' moment involves each individual learner incorporating new information into, and making connections with, their existing understanding and view of the world. Learning is therefore an active process – a product of doing rather than receiving.

Learning involves building on existing understanding

> 'Understanding is related to the ability to make valid connections between existing knowledge and experiences with that of new inputs.'

John Abbot, President of the 21st Century Learning Initiative

It is difficult for an individual to make sense of information if they have no prior knowledge. It is hard to make connections if there is nothing to connect to. It means that learning cannot take place if it is too far removed from an individual's current reality. *'Start from what they know'* is widely accepted as good practice in the classroom.

Zone of proximal development

The Russian psychologist Lev Vygotsky argues that children learn in what he terms the zone of proximal development (ZPD). This is the area just beyond the child's current capabilities, which he or she cannot quite master alone.

The child is, however, capable of functioning at this level with the aid of support. As the child develops, the support can be reduced until, eventually, he or she is able to operate at the same level independently. Thus a child learns gradually to do things unaided that previously could only be done with support.

The support, which is often referred to as 'scaffolding', is provided both by the teacher and other students, and takes the form of interaction and teacher intervention.

Successful scaffolding requires:

- frequent, high quality teacher–student and student–student interactions

- that students are able to verbalize their thinking

- that teachers ask open-ended questions

- that teacher interventions probe, challenge, extend and help clarify the thinking of the student.

Learning takes place at a level just beyond current understanding

The area just beyond current understanding is described by the Russian psychologist Lev Vygotsky as the zone of proximal development (ZPD). The ZPD extends just beyond a child's current capabilities – it is a level that the child cannot quite master alone. He or she is, however, capable of functioning at this level with the aid of support. This support, which is often referred to as 'scaffolding', is provided by both the teacher and other students. As the child develops, the support can be reduced until, eventually, he or she is able to operate at the same level independently. Thus a child learns gradually to do things unaided that previously could only be done with support.

Implications for schools

A conscious and genuine commitment to understanding will inevitably have an impact on the way in which we teach. Understanding is not inevitable. Just because it has been taught does not necessarily mean that it has been learned. Understanding is the result of cognitive activity – thinking. It therefore demands an approach to lessons that actively engages students in the learning process with the emphasis, in the classroom, not on *transferring* information, but on helping students *make sense* of it.

However, in recent years, teachers have faced the twinned pressures of ever increasing accountability and a content-heavy curriculum, with content rather than pedagogy often assuming centre stage. Not surprisingly, the emphasis in many classrooms has been on delivering, as opposed to exploring, the curriculum.

When this happens, there is a genuine danger that children leave classrooms having failed to understand the work they have been doing. A syllabus may have been covered, information may have been transferred, but if it hasn't been understood, it hasn't been learned. Part of the problem is that it is so easy to be fooled. Much can masquerade as learning. Pages of notes, particularly when they have been written neatly, and successfully completed comprehension exercises can be a convincing disguise. Consider the example below, taken from a comprehension exercise in history.

'The reason for Harold's defeat was a complex combination of factors including his own tactical mistakes and William's military strategy ...'

Question: What caused Harold's defeat?

Answer: The reason for Harold's defeat was a complex combination of factors, including his own tactical mistakes and William's military strategy.

Teachers support and guide students through the learning process, engaging them through:

- **tasks**

- **interactions**

It is therefore the nature and quality of these tasks and interactions that is the key to high quality teaching and learning.

Engaging the learner

Although understanding requires individuals to make personal sense of information, it does not require them to do so in isolation. Indeed, Vygotsky emphasizes the point that learning is often the result of interaction with both the teacher and fellow students.

Teachers play a pivotal role in the learning process, guiding, supporting and prompting students in a way that both challenges and shapes thinking and deepens understanding. Above all, they engage learners – the nature and quality of this engagement holding the key to how much of a lesson is learned.

Teachers engage learners in two ways:

- **through tasks and activities**
- **through interaction and intervention.**

Tasks

It is the quality and nature of the tasks that often distinguish satisfactory from excellent lessons and largely determine the extent to which information will be understood. Learning involves creating personal meaning. This must be reflected in the nature of the task, the emphasis being on re-creating rather than simply reproducing information. In particular, tasks must do three things:

- *develop* understanding
- allow the learner to *demonstrate* his or her understanding
- allow the teacher to *assess* understanding.

Interaction

The purpose of teacher interaction and intervention is to support students' learning by probing and shaping their thinking and helping them to clarify and extend their understanding. It is considerably different from interactions that limit the learner to playing 'guess what the teacher's thinking'. High quality interactions that support learning require:

- frequent teacher–student and student–student interactions
- frequent opportunities for students to verbalize their thinking
- teachers asking open-ended questions
- interventions that probe, challenge, extend and help clarify thinking.

The nature of high quality interactions and tasks is explored in greater depth on pages 107 and 111.

Where will your next '5%' come from?

To what extent will it come from students who:

- could, but don't believe they can?
- could, but don't want to?

State, style and structure

State, style and structure are the keys to effective learning.

- People learn best when they are in an appropriate physical and emotional state to learn. Learning is optimized when the brain is nourished and students are relaxed, confident and motivated.

- People learn best in different ways. For maximum progress, people must have frequent opportunities to work in their preferred learning style.

- Mature, successful learners progress through discrete phases of learning quite naturally. Lessons should be structured to reflect these phases and guide young, immature learners through the learning process.

State

> **'For learners to learn, they must first be in the appropriate state for learning.'**

Eric Jensen

You can have the best textbooks, the most expensive computer suite and the most up-to-date resources, but if the students are not in the right state and really don't want to learn, even the best teacher will struggle. If our job is to help children learn, then our first task must be to ensure that they are in an appropriate state. It is not an optional extra; it is a necessary precursor to learning, for it is only when they are alert and receptive that students will make sense of and retain the information coming their way.

Learners must be in an appropriate physical and emotional state to learn. Physical and emotional states are linked: a lack of breakfast, for example, will affect mood, concentration and memory.

1 **Physical**

- **The brain needs *fuel* – water, oxygen and glucose – to function efficiently.**

2 **Emotional**

- **Students need to be *relaxed*. Negative stress impairs or even prevents learning.**
- **People must believe that they can learn. *Self-esteem* plays an important role in learning.**
- ***Motivation* is key. People learn best when they *want* to learn.**

Water

There are schools where children:

- do not have access to clean drinking water during the day
- are not allowed to drink water in the classroom
- are allowed to drink water in the classroom*
- are positively encouraged to drink water in the classroom.*

* health and safety permitting

Oxygen

Increasing numbers of schools are employing Brain Gym® to help get students in an appropriate state to learn. Brain Gym® is a series of exercises devised by Paul and Gail Dennison. The exercises can be used in a number of ways:

- by an educational kinesiologist, working with individual students in an attempt to unblock specific learning difficulties
- with groups of students as a warm-up session before a lesson, or as a 'state-break' activity during a lesson.

Food

- Some schools have breakfast bars. Some don't.
- Some schools provide bowls of grapes and raisins for children to 'graze' on during the day. Some don't.

We know that water, oxygen and the right sort of nourishment are crucial to brain function and therefore learning. What does *your* school do about it?

Physical state

Water

The brain, which is 90 per cent water, requires water to function properly. Water conducts the tiny electrical currents that drive the brain, removes waste and toxins from the body and allows significantly more oxygen to bind in red blood cells. As a rule of thumb, we need about eight tumblers of water each day and up to three times as much when we are under stress. When we are dehydrated, learning is impaired as mood and concentration deteriorate.

Oxygen

The brain uses around 20 per cent of the body's oxygen intake. In oxygen terms, it is the greediest organ in the body. When the heart rate slows – for example, when we sit down for a long period – less freshly oxygenated blood feeds the brain, reducing brain efficiency.

Breakfast

The link between breakfast and mood is well established. Concentration, behaviour, memory and of course learning are affected when the brain receives inappropriate or insufficient fuel. Many students arrive at school without an adequate breakfast, and are therefore on the back foot before the day has even begun.

Emotional state

Relaxed alert

The human brain does not learn effectively when placed under negative stress. While a degree of stress will do no harm – a little stress can actually heighten concentration and improve learning – too much negative stress will impair or, in extreme cases, prevent learning.

Under stress, the instinctive and emotional centres of the brain dominate and override rational logical thought. It is the natural default process of the brain that is part of our inbuilt survival response. When threatened, we prepare to fight or flee. Chemical changes take place in our bodies in preparation for responding to the threat – an advantage when fighting or fleeing an enemy, but less helpful when trying to learn!

This 'override mechanism' is triggered by different things in each individual. However, as a rule of thumb, if something causes you stress, your body will react. We have no control over it. It is an automatic physiological response. Tests, being asked a question in public, or being 'put on the spot' are causes of considerable anxiety for many students. Often this anxiety is particularly acute in certain subjects or with particular teachers. Not only will students fail to learn when in a stressed state, they will often respond in a defensive or aggressive manner designed to detract attention from the thing that is causing the stress.

People learn best in 'high challenge–low stress' environments, when the brain is in a state often described as 'relaxed alert'. Students invariably respond to a challenge. No self-respecting teenage boy can reject the 'I bet you can't' gauntlet! The problem for the teacher in the classroom is that, while there is a massive difference between challenge and stress, there is only a thin dividing line, with each student drawing it in a different place. Activities that challenge one student intimidate another.

Consider these opening sentences from two different school brochures:

- 'Children cannot be good at everything. At this school we seek to provide an extensive range of opportunities so that each child can find an area in which they excel.'

- 'At our school all children are good at everything – just to varying degrees.'

Creating a high challenge–low stress learning environment is not always easy, but it is necessary if students are going to learn effectively. Learning often involves taking a risk and extending your current boundaries – there are huge parallels here with teachers developing new approaches to their classroom practice. People of any age are unlikely to take that risk if they don't feel comfortable and secure.

Positive beliefs

Believing that you will succeed, or at least have a chance of being successful, is one of the foundation stones necessary for successful learning.

Yet negative beliefs surround us.

- 'I can't do that'
- 'I'm no good at French'
- 'I go to pieces in exams'

Such comments are frequently heard in schools. The problem is that *expectations* inform *outcomes*. If a student *believes* that he will fail, he probably will. It is a barrier to learning that even the most successful teacher will struggle to overcome.

Negative beliefs are generated from within. Often they are based on flimsy evidence and are the result of the way in which an individual interprets the subtle messages received from families, friends and teachers. Sometimes these beliefs are firmly in place before a child reaches school – 'We're no good at sport in this family' – sometimes they have their origin in the classroom.

Ben was just four when he returned home from school and announced that he was no good at drawing. To this day he is reluctant to draw. Michael – now a successful businessman – will tell you that he can't do maths. He will also tell you that it was his teacher who informed him that he was 'useless' at the subject. Fiona will tell you that she can't sing – she recalls torturous music lessons from her schooldays when she was forced to stand at the back and play the triangle.

Think of something that you cannot do.

Where were you when you decided that you couldn't do it?

Think back to the best teacher you had as a child.

Almost certainly, he or she:

- made you feel special

- treated you with respect

- took an interest in you as an individual

- convinced you that he or she believed in your ability

- conveyed a genuine sense of enjoyment and enthusiasm

- made lessons interesting and learning fun.

In other words, the teacher managed to exert a positive influence on your motivation and self-esteem.

How did he or she manage to do this?

What did he or she do that the others didn't?

Quite probably, it wasn't much. But it was highly significant.

Three things are worth considering.

1　Teachers have a powerful influence over a student's perception of his or her ability. Although we have no control over the messages that children receive from their parents and friends, everything that teachers do and say in the classroom will challenge or reinforce a child's belief about his or her ability to learn.

2　The judgements that fuel negative beliefs are based upon the individual's *interpretation* of experiences. Michael's maths teacher may be horrified to learn that he was responsible for Michael's negative attitude towards the subject. Like all teachers, he was probably doing his utmost to motivate and reassure the young boy. However, irrespective of motive, his words and actions had a negative effect. It is the interpretation of the message rather than the intention behind it that makes the impact.

3　Negative beliefs have a nasty habit of getting blown out of proportion. Michael is a businessman. He can add, subtract, calculate percentages and perform many other mathematical functions. Yet he believes that he can't do maths! The reality is that he struggles with *aspects* of the subject. Similarly, although Fiona will tell you that she can't sing, in fact she can – she just sings out of tune!

Wherever they come from, however illogical they are and however exaggerated they become, negative beliefs are a massive barrier to learning for a great many people. It is particularly sad that so many young people fail to do themselves justice in formal examinations simply because they are in a negative frame of mind and a totally inappropriate emotional state when they enter the exam hall.

Motivation

> 'The three most important factors in learning are motivation, motivation and motivation.'

Sir Christopher Ball

People learn best when they want to learn. People learn best when they are desperate to learn. It makes motivation the cornerstone of the entire learning process.

And yet how many teachers have encountered a student or a class who are bored, who can't see the relevance of what they are being asked to do and who are making it clear that they really don't want to be there?

Working with students who clearly have the ability but who lack the desire to learn is one of the most frustrating aspects of being a teacher. On occasions it feels that no matter how hard you work, how meticulously you prepare and how imaginative the lessons, there are still students who display a 'couldn't care less' attitude. It is an uphill struggle from the outset.

Imagine how it would be if students were arriving at your room eager to learn and desperate to achieve.

Does your school have a Head of Motivation?
If the answer is 'no', what made you decide that you didn't need one?

- Do you have a motivation policy and/or a self-esteem recovery programme?
- Have your staff received any motivation training?

Few schools nationally have a Head of Motivation. Few teachers have received specialist motivation training. As a nation, we are effectively leaving the most significant factor in learning to chance.

Implications for schools

- Few would dispute that motivation and self-esteem hold the key to learning. Yet how many schools have a Head of Motivation? This is a whole-school issue – does it not demand a whole-school response?

- Although the emotional state of the learner undeniably exerts a considerable influence over the quality of learning and levels of attainment of individual students, it is a variable that teachers and schools do not control. We do not control it because we do not own it. Motivation and self-esteem belong to the individual. However, while we do not control it, we can influence the emotional state of our students. Indeed we cannot help but influence it. Everything that we do and say in the classroom, consciously or inadvertently, will have an influence on our students, positive or otherwise.

- The influences upon motivation and self-esteem are often small and subtle. Frequently they operate at a subconscious level. Little things can make a big difference to mood and outlook. This is particularly encouraging, as it sometimes seems that our influence is greatly outweighed by potentially negative messages that children receive from outside school. In many respects the steps that teachers and schools take in this area appear to be a 'drop in the ocean'. But, to paraphrase Mother Theresa's famous reply, the important thing is that we are putting drops in the right ocean. And enough drops will begin to make a difference.

- How much 'motivation training' do teachers receive? For many teachers the answer would be 'not much' or even 'none whatsoever'. This is not to suggest that teachers do not do their utmost to motivate and reassure. Of course they do. We all can identify teachers who, through a combination of personality, philosophy and approach, inspire, reassure and generally exert a positive influence over the students they teach. Many of them, however, are unsure of precisely *how* they have such a positive influence, much of what they do being instinctive and intuitive – a subconscious response and approach that has been moulded over many years in the classroom. Yet if we do not operate at a conscious level and pinpoint the precise words and actions that have such a positive impact:

  1 how do we ensure that all teachers are using them? Consistency of message is crucial in developing self-esteem

  2 what do we say to newcomers to the school or profession? Do we leave new teachers to serve 5–10 years and work out for themselves how to motivate students?

  3 how do we ensure that our words and actions are having the desired, positive effect? If little things can make a big difference, little things can also be potentially very harmful.

The power of language

If little things can make a big difference, little things can also do a lot of damage. It is easy for teachers to have a negative impact upon the emotional state of a student, without intending to or realizing what they have done.

Consider the examples below.

How many times do you hear teachers saying 'All you've got to do now is …' The intention clearly is to reassure. Yet how many students translate this into 'Oh no, I must be really thick if I can't even do this one'. All of them? Some of them? One of them? Do you know which one?

How many times do teachers tell students that they don't care?

'Fiona, can you put down your pen please.'
'I'm just finishing off the work.'
*'**I don't care** what you're doing, you need to be listening to me.'*

'Gareth, can you stop that please.'
'Other teachers let us.'
*' **I don't care** what other teachers do.'*

The phrase 'I don't care' is frequently heard in classrooms. A better alternative is the phrase 'maybe … and'.

'I was just finishing off the work.'
*'**Maybe** you were **and** I need you to listen to me for a few minutes while I explain the next bit.'*

'Other teachers let us.'
*'**Maybe** they do **and** you know the rule in this classroom.'*

Few teachers are born using phrases such as 'maybe … and'. Few people can think of them on the spur of the moment. However, they can be learned as part of a whole-school approach to motivation and self-esteem.

For further information on the power of language, see any of the books by Peter Hook and Andy Vass recommended on page 261.

- There is a genuine danger that teachers and schools, despite the best of intentions, can actually have a negative impact on a child's confidence and motivation. If we do not know where we are putting our 'drops', some may inadvertently go in the 'wrong ocean'. Consider the box below.

> A Year 9 student is quoted in John MacBeath's book *Schools Must Speak for Themselves* as saying:
>
> > 'I used to feel that this school cared about how well I was doing. Now I just think the only thing it cares about is how well *it's* doing.'
>
> What had given the student this impression? It almost certainly wasn't intentional. Again, it is the *interpretation* not the intention of the message that is significant.
>
> How many schools celebrate success? How many schools acknowledge and celebrate that 'a record number of students achieved level 3', or '… level 5', or '… five GCSEs at grades A*–C'? How does that sit with the centrality of individual recognition and belonging as a key influence on self-esteem? As one young girl once said:
>
> > 'I don't care that I'm part of the most successful cohort there's ever been – I care about me!'

- All schools have a policy designed to influence the state of the students. It is a behaviour policy. Behaviour is important; it is unlikely that students will learn effectively unless the teacher establishes a calm and orderly atmosphere conducive to learning. Schools have a behaviour policy because the issue is too important to be left to chance; if students are not well behaved they're unlikely to learn. But if they're not motivated, they're unlikely to learn either. Why then do we leave the motivation of students to chance – to the experience, common sense and intuition of individual teachers? Why do we not address *motivation* as part of a wider school approach to ensuring, or at least making it more likely, that students are in an appropriate state to learn?

- Even the best teachers can become more effective by adding a strategy or two to their repertoire. However, the teachers who we really wish to move are those who deliver competent lessons but fail to inspire and motivate students. It is within this group that both the capacity to change and improve, and the need to do so, is the greatest. While we cannot fundamentally alter teachers' personalities, nor, in many cases, shift their philosophy, we can equip them with a range of strategies. There are no guarantees, but by highlighting motivation and self-esteem as a key issue, we make it *more likely* that all teachers will approach teaching in a manner that brings out the best of their students.

Do you adopt a systematic, whole-school approach to accommodating the individual learning styles of your students?

- **If not, what made you decide that you didn't need to?**

- **If so, what made you adopt your particular approach?**

Style

People learn best in different ways; learning will be enhanced when students have frequent opportunities to learn in their preferred style. Although people can learn outside of their preferred style, a significant mismatch between the way in which a student learns best and the way in which he or she is being taught can easily result in boredom, lack of motivation and underachievement.

All school leaders need to be aware of the impact that individual learning preferences can have in the classroom. It is an important area – an issue far too important to be ignored – and not surprisingly, there is growing interest in the notion of learning style around the globe. It is also, however, an area that is easy to oversimplify. The problem is that there are many different ways in which learning styles can be classified, with thinking and research in this area developing all the time. One of the most useful summaries of this whole field, and the implications for schools and teachers, can be found in Paul Ginnis' excellent book, *The Teacher's Toolkit*, and it is highly recommended that all school leaders find time to read it.

Ginnis suggests that the many different learning style classifications can be grouped into seven main types. Three of the most useful approaches for schools are classifications that refer to the way in which people prefer to *receive* information, classifications that are broadly based on how people prefer to *process* information, and Howard Gardner's multiple intelligence theory, which centres on his belief that individuals have a range of talents and strengths and are therefore intelligent in different ways. In reality, our individual approach to learning, or learning style, is a complex combination of all these systems.

Our individual learning style is a combination of:

- how we prefer to receive information
- how we prefer to process information
- the ways in which we are 'intelligent'.

Receiving information

Some people prefer to see information. These people are often referred to as 'visual learners'. Some people prefer to hear information – these are sometime called 'auditory learners' – while 'kinesthetic learners' learn best by moving, touching and doing.

This VAK (visual/auditory/kinesthetic) classification is one of the most frequently used methods of determining learning styles in schools. It is a useful system, not least because it deals with the way in which people prefer to receive sensory information, and as teachers we have a high degree of control over how we choose to transmit such information. However, it should be acknowledged that the classification has some limitations and should not be applied too rigidly. For example:

- some visual learners prefer to see text-based information while others prefer learning from pictures and diagrams
- the umbrella term 'kinesthetic learner' refers to three different types of learner – students who are particularly tactile and learn effectively from activities such as handling artefacts or sequencing cards, students who need to be moving around (for example, in role-play type activities) and, finally, kinesthetic internal learners who are the students who empathize and relate particularly well to stories and emotional experiences

Learning styles grid

	Sequential processor				Random processor
Visual					
Auditory	Linguistic **Josie**	Logical–mathe-matical	Visual–spatial	Musical	
	Bodily-kines-thetic	Intra-personal	Inter-personal	Naturalist	
Kinesthetic					

An individual's learning style is a complex combination of the way he or she prefers to receive information, the way he or she prefers to process it and the ways in which he or she is particularly 'intelligent'.

This combination can be plotted on a grid such as the one above. All six boxes can be further subdivided to take account of multiple intelligences.

In the example above, Josie is predominately an auditory learner, who prefers to process information in a sequential manner. Her dominant intelligence is linguistic.

The grid can be used to plot the learning preferences of both teachers and students. A significant mismatch between the way in which teachers prefer to learn (this will probably be reflected in the way they teach) and the way in which students would prefer to learn could well be a contributory cause of underachievement, boredom, demotivation and poor behaviour.

- it is misleading to refer to an individual as a 'visual learner'. We are combinations of VAK – not V, A or K but V, A and K! We each have a different profile and our preferred way of receiving information may vary with circumstance. For example, you may prefer to hear rather than read a proposal, yet prefer to see a map than receive spoken directions.

Translators

Neuro-Linguistic Programming (NLP) expert Michael Grinder claims that, while most people are sufficiently multisensory to learn outside of their preferred sensory channel, a small number of students (about 20 per cent) will have such a strong preference for receiving information in a particular way that they will not learn effectively outside of their preferred style.

Grinder refers to these students as 'translators' – as they receive sensory information, they have to translate it into their preferred mode before they can make sense of it. For example, when a highly visual student hears a piece of information, he or she will need to create a visual image in the brain.

Translators are faced with a major problem in the classroom as while they are translating information they will miss the next thing that is being said and end up with significant gaps in their knowledge. Michael Grinder suggests that over 65 per cent of re-teaching time (this is different from time spent reinforcing or reviewing) is spent with translators.

Processing information

Some people process information in a sequential, logical manner, while others naturally process randomly and intuitively. Logical, linear processors will often feel uncomfortable if they feel that a learning experience lacks structure, while random, intuitive processors can easily feel restricted by an orderly sequential approach to learning.

There are a number of classifications that determine whether an individual is essentially a random or a sequential processor. Determining hemispheric dominance is as useful an approach as any. The two hemispheres of the neo-cortex of the brain process information in different ways. The logic hemisphere – for most people the left – processes in a linear, logical way, concentrating upon details and components of the whole. The gestalt hemisphere – usually the right – processes in a random, intuitive manner, focusing upon the overview or big picture.

Although it is now generally accepted that the two hemispheres do not operate in isolation and that both are involved in virtually all thinking activity, we each have a *dominant* hemisphere that becomes particularly pronounced in times of stress. For many people, this dominance is only slight, but for some people, it is particularly significant. The problem often comes in the classroom when a teacher with a strong dominance and preference for a particular style of processing encounters a student with an equally strong, but opposite, dominance.

Multiple intelligences

1 Linguistic	the ability to manipulate words effectively
2 Logical–mathematical	the ability to reason, and to see patterns and relationships
3 Visual–spatial	the ability to visualize easily and feel comfortable with graphs and maps
4 Musical	the ability to discern patterns in sound, including a well-developed sense of rhythm
5 Bodily-kinesthetic	the skilful use of the body
6 Intrapersonal	the ability to know oneself
7 Interpersonal	the ability to get on well with other people
8 Naturalist	the ability to make distinctions in the natural world and to recognize flora and fauna

Many people have built upon Gardner's original work, arguing that it does not go far enough. For example, there are people who suggest that 'visual' and 'spatial' should be considered as two separate forms of intelligence. Others would claim that discrete and worthy forms of intelligence are omitted, such as 'inventive intelligence' (those people who are particularly creative).

Multiple intelligences

First postulated by Howard Gardner in 1983, multiple intelligence theory is composed of two key elements.

1   Intelligence is not fixed. It can and does change throughout an individual's life. A single IQ measurement is therefore meaningless.

2   There are different types of intelligences. We all possess each type to various degrees in what amounts to our 'personal intelligence profile'.

Gardner originally identified seven intelligences, before adding 'naturalist', to make a total of eight, and argued that the formal school system in both the USA and the UK favoured just two – those who were good with words (linguistic intelligence) and those who were good with numbers and problems (logical–mathematical intelligence). Schools tend to favour students who are strong in these areas, in the ways in which they are both taught and assessed.

Help students learn about multiple intelligences

Making students aware that there are many different forms of intelligence can have a powerful effect on their self-esteem and attitude towards learning. The multiple intelligences model can be used to help each child both recognize and value his or her particular strengths and talents. It can also form the basis for any self-esteem policy – there can be nothing more important for schools and teachers than to find out what students are good at and let them know that we know.

Help students learn through multiple intelligences

The real value of the multiple intelligences model, however, extends far beyond the obvious – children who are strong in the area of musical intelligence will excel in music while students who are logical–mathematical will be good at maths. Learning is enhanced when students have frequent opportunities to learn in their dominant intelligence irrespective of curriculum area. This means that, while someone who is musically talented but whose logical–mathematical intelligence is not particularly strong may never be terrific at maths, he or she will be significantly *better* if able to use that musical intelligence in the maths classroom.

Critics

There are those who do not accept Gardner's multiple intelligences model. There are those who argue that he overstates the case. Yet before 1983, long before anyone had heard the phrase 'multiple intelligences', it was apparent that people were different. There were always children who were good at geography but struggled in French and children who were musically gifted but found maths unfathomable.

Gardner's model drew attention to the range of abilities possessed by children who were previously branded as failures by a narrow system, and offered students the possibility of learning more effectively if they were able to utilize a personal strength, even in a curriculum area that was a relative weakness.

Whether you call them 'intelligences' or 'strengths' – and the debate will surely go on and on – it is hard to deny that individuals are talented in different ways. What we call their talents is not important. Recognizing, valuing, nurturing and utilizing them, and helping students to do the same, is.

Determine the range of learning styles among your staff

Ask each member of staff to determine his or her own learning style and position on the grid on page 70.

(Many people will instinctively know their preferred learning style. A range of questionnaires and indicators can be found in the recommended reading on page 260 for those people who are unsure.)

- As an individual, reflect on your position on the grid. To what extent does the way you teach reflect the way in which you learn?

- What is the distribution of the entire staff?

- Ask teachers who share a similar profile to identify three things that they find particularly helpful and three things they find irritating when they are learning. Share this information with the entire staff.

- Do teachers of a particular subject share a similar learning style? Is this reflected in the way they teach? Does this mean that students with a significantly different learning style are in danger of being disadvantaged in this subject?

- Do teachers of the same subject have very different preferred learning styles? Does this mean that students will be taught in a different way depending on which teacher they get?

- Use staff as a resource. Plot the position of each teacher on the grid on page 70 and display it in the staffroom. When you are having trouble with a student, seek out a colleague who has a similar learning style and find out the things they find helpful or irritating when learning.

Implications for schools

● People learn best when they have frequent opportunities to learn in their preferred style. However, it should be acknowledged that people can learn outside of their preferred approach. Kinesthetic learners can read! The issue is about how people *prefer* to learn and how they learn best. There are two likely consequences when students are frequently required to work in a way that is alien to their natural instincts:

  1 a *direct* impact on learning – students will almost certainly learn more effectively if able to work to their strengths

  2 an *indirect* impact – students are more likely to be bored and demotivated, and to misbehave, if constantly asked to work in a way that they don't enjoy.

● Some subject areas will favour certain types of learner by the very nature of the subject. For example, kinesthetic learners will have more opportunities to learn in their preferred style in PE or technology than they will in history or maths. Students whose dominant intelligence is logical–mathematical are likely to enjoy and excel in maths. Students who are musically gifted are likely to do well in music.

● The preferred learning style of a teacher is likely to influence the way in which he or she teaches. For example, a teacher who is a linear, logical thinker is likely to adopt a sequential, structured approach to lessons. While students who are also linear thinkers will be comfortable with this approach, random, intuitive processors could find the approach unnecessarily restrictive and could easily become bored.

This situation is exacerbated when the learning preference and, therefore, teaching approach of the teacher is particularly extreme. Even when a teacher does not have a strong learning preference and adopts a fairly balanced approach to teaching, his or her natural tendencies are likely to emerge during times of increased stress – for example, when faced with pressure to cover a syllabus in a short period of time.

● Schools, by their very nature, favour particular kinds of learner. Students who are logic hemisphere dominant and predominantly visual and auditory learners – the ones who sit still, listen attentively and can follow simple instructions – tend to do well in school, their preferred approach being well suited to the structured, orderly environment of the classroom.

The students who are most challenging to teach are those who are random, intuitive processors or kinesthetic learners. Put the two together and we have a combination that many teachers find difficult to deal with in the classroom. These are the students who are often disadvantaged in schools, not least because they have significantly fewer opportunities to work in their preferred style. Not surprisingly, many of these students become bored and demotivated. Sadly, many end up as significant discipline problems, their natural desire to move consistently landing them in trouble for what is often termed 'low-level disruption'.

'If students are allowed always to work within their preferred style, they will remain narrow and ill-equipped. On the other hand, if they are forced too early or too often to work in non-preferred and uncomfortable ways, they are bound to underachieve and may well become alienated.'

Paul Ginnis

Meeting the challenge

The significance of individual learning preferences demands a response from each and every school. The extreme response would be to determine how students learn best and then teach them accordingly. It is an understandable temptation. However, many would argue that it is an unnecessary and even unhelpful strategy. Consider the following.

- The issue is about learning *preferences*. So-called 'auditory learners' can read! Learning is best done through multisensory experiences with all children being given frequent opportunities to hear, see *and* do.

- To be successful in later life, students will have to be able to adapt to learn in a variety of circumstances and in different ways. A one-dimensional approach during the school years will do little to develop their ability to learn in a variety of styles.

- The evidence on which children are grouped is often spurious. Frequently, a questionnaire is used to determine a child's preferred learning style. Used cautiously, such questionnaires can be a useful tool and give an indication of the way in which a child prefers to learn. However, they vary enormously in quality and accuracy and should be viewed as providing an indicator of preference rather than the definitive 'answer'.

- Students are often grouped on the basis of just one classification. One of the most common ways of distinguishing between learning styles is on the basis of VAK. However, learning styles are a complex combination of different classifications and for some students the way in which they receive sensory information is largely inconsequential. Take Sam, for example. He has no strong preference about the way in which he receives sensory information but does have a strong preference for random processing. If he is required to work in a tightly structured manner he will be irritated and uncomfortable, irrespective of whether he is in the visual, auditory or kinesthetic group.

There is, however, a counter argument. Broadly grouping students by learning preference simply reduces the scale of the challenge facing teachers. It is a little like grouping children by ability. Teachers know that even in a top set there will be children of varying ability; however, the challenge is more manageable. When children are grouped by learning preference there will still be differences in preferred ways of working, which will vary with circumstances, but the range of learning styles will have been reduced.

Even in such groups, learning can still be multisensory with students being encouraged to develop their ability to learn outside of their preferred mode. However, the *emphasis* can be placed firmly upon working in a way that suits the majority of the students. Thus a group of students with a preference for learning kinesthetically will still be required to read and listen, but will be given frequent opportunities to move and learn by doing.

Meeting the challenge

- Find out how you normally teach. Are there any types of learner disadvantaged by this approach? Consider more than one classification of learning style – this is a complex area.

- Focus on students causing concern – students who are underachieving, badly behaved or demotivated. To what extent is a mismatch between the way in which these students would prefer to learn and the way they are required to work contributing to these concerns?

- Devote time to identifying and sharing strategies that would appeal to different types of learner. Develop a resource bank of good ideas.

- Systematically build a variety of learning styles into all schemes of work. Design an appropriate pro-forma. Make it school policy.

- Ensure that each type of learner has at least one opportunity to work in their preferred style during every unit of work.

- Use learning styles as a basis for lesson observation. Evaluate the quality of the learning experience for particular types of learner.

There is clearly no single best model – individual circumstance and context will have a big bearing upon how schools plan to meet the challenge of accommodating many different types of learner. However, it is a challenge that must be met if learning is to be optimized.

In determining a strategy, four factors are crucial.

1 Keep it in perspective! This is about learning *preferences*. We are all multisensory learners.

2 A balance must be established between giving students frequent opportunities to work in their preferred style and developing their ability to work in ways that don't always come naturally to them.

3 Keep it manageable. The strategy must be practical and realistic, given the constraints and realities of the classroom.

4 Where are you now? Some schools are already grouping students by their learning preference and writing schemes of work around individual learning styles. Other schools are not yet at this stage.

A suggested approach

1 Determine the way in which teachers approach lessons

Start by establishing the way in which teachers tend to approach lessons and which types of learner are advantaged or disadvantaged as a result. It is an activity that can be completed by individual teachers or curriculum areas. There are a number of ways of approaching this exercise.

● Analyse schemes of work or lesson plans. Use different coloured highlighter pens to highlight opportunities for visual, auditory and kinesthetic learners, different types of multiple intelligences, and random and sequential processors.

● Use lesson observations to establish the range and frequency of opportunities for different types of learner. Evaluate lessons against learning styles. For example, lessons are often judged as 'good' or 'satisfactory' – but for whom? For kinesthetic learners? For random processors? Use the data as a basis for self-reflection or discussion workshops.

● Use the grid on page 70 to identify the learning styles of individual teachers. To what extent are their preferences reflected in the way in which they teach?

2 Identify the students who are causing you concern

This is a realistic way of approaching the challenge of learning styles and a particularly effective place to start if the school is in the early stages of tackling this issue. Instead of trying to determine the learning style of every student – in large schools this is a particularly daunting task – concentrate upon the ones who are not learning effectively at the present.

There are two ways of focusing on students causing concern. Again, this activity can be completed by individual teachers or as a department.

1 List the ten students who irritate you the most. Identify those whose behaviour, attendance and motivation are a cause for concern. Is their poor behaviour and lack of motivation consistent across the curriculum, or are there subjects where the problems are particularly acute?

- Does your school have an equal opportunities policy?

- Does it include an entitlement for all students to have frequent opportunities to work in their preferred learning style?

- Does your school have a commitment to inclusion? How is this reflected in the way in which you teach?

2   Identify students who are underachieving. This can be based upon a gut feeling (all teachers can identify students who could be doing that little bit better) or by analysing the available data.

Once these students have been identified, consider these questions.

● Where do these students appear on the grid on page 70?

● How do their positions compare with the positions of the staff teaching them?

● Is there a link between the personal learning styles of the students causing concern and the way in which they are being required to work?

● What could be done to achieve a closer match between the way these students would prefer to learn and the way in which they are currently being taught?

3   Provide variety and choice

Variety and choice are the key to meeting individual learning preferences. However, variety and choice don't just happen – they have to be planned for. Even when teachers are aware of the need to cater for a variety of learning styles, even when they are committed to doing so, they do not always do so. The best of intentions do not always materialize in teachers employing a range of learning strategies, for at least two reasons.

1   Most people are not aware of the kinds of activities that would appeal to learners with significantly different learning preferences to their own.

2   Most teachers will fall back on their familiar, preferred approach to teaching when they are placed under pressure – for example, when they become tired towards the end of term or when they have to cover a large amount of the syllabus in a limited amount of time.

Providing variety and choice in the classroom involves:

● identifying and sharing strategies that appeal to different types of learners

● systematically including them in schemes of work and lesson plans. Basing schemes of work around learning styles does not guarantee that all teachers will include a variety of activities in their lessons, but it does make it more likely

● devoting planning time (meeting time or time on INSET days) to generating a range of learning strategies that appeal to different types of learner. Develop a resource bank of strategies for kinesthetic learners, good ideas for random processors, and so on

● utilizing the range of learning styles of the staff. Go outside of your curriculum area to identify generic strategies. Make sure all staff are aware of the learning and teaching styles of their colleagues – use them as a resource. The grid on page 70 will reveal their learning preferences. If you want to ask someone who is a kinesthetic learner, random processor and has well-developed interpersonal skills the kinds of activities that help him or her learn, you now know who to ask!

● attaching non-specialists to curriculum areas during planning sessions. We are seeking to be creative and approach lessons from a different angle. Imagine what a maths lesson planned by a musician, technology teacher, drama specialist and historian would look like (page 172)!

Where does your next '5%' come from?

To what extent will it come from students who could do it, if only they were given a chance to do it in a different way?

- developing a school approach to writing schemes of work that includes reference to learning styles. Involve the entire staff in designing a suitable pro-forma based around multiple intelligences, VAK, random vs sequential processing, and so on.

- making it a school policy that there will be at least one opportunity for each type of learner to learn in his or her preferred style, in every unit of work. Of course, our ultimate goal is for *all* students to be able to learn in their preferred style *every* lesson – a minimum of once per unit is a start.

Useful strategies for the classroom

Three quick and easy-to-use strategies to accommodate different types of learner in the classroom are described below.

Transformation

Transformation is an extremely effective learning activity in its own right (see *Strategies for Closing the Learning Gap*, page 201). It simply involves the learner having to change the form of the information presented to them during a lesson. For example, students could be asked to portray a piece of text in diagrammatic form, or produce a written description of a graph. When we ask students to transform information, we significantly increase the chances of:

1 engaging and linking both hemispheres of the neo-cortex (for example, when keywords are put to music the logic hemisphere will process the lyrics while the gestalt hemisphere processes the tune)

2 introducing a kinesthetic dimension into learning (for example, role-playing a quadratic equation or the life of a cell, or miming a poem)

3 allowing students to learn through their dominant intelligence (for example, converting a formula into a rap, or describing the slave trade to the tune of *One man went to mow*).

Choice

Providing choice of learning activity is one of the most effective ways of accommodating different types of learner. Not only are students making a positive 'I want to' statement, they are also significantly more likely to be able to work in a way that suits them.

The choice can be open ('How would you like to show that information?' or 'How are you planning to tackle that problem?') or guided ('Would you like to write a short description, draw a labelled diagram, produce a flow chart, turn it into a cartoon strip, put the keywords to music or in a poem, or use the equipment on your desk to make a simple model? Your choice.')

Open-ended tasks and problem solving

Problem-solving activities can usually be approached in a variety of ways. Some learners will choose to tackle the exercise in a step-by-step logical fashion, while other students will adopt a more trial-and-error, instinctive approach. One way is no more effective than another and different types of learner will be able to work in the way that suits them best. Try to build at least one such activity into every unit of work.

Lessons should reflect the way in which the brain learns

- Learning involves building on existing knowledge.

- The brain will more readily absorb detail when it can place it in a wider context.

- The brain will notice things that it has been primed to look for.

- People have limited concentration spans.

- People remember more from the beginning and end of an experience.

- The brain cycles between receiving information and making sense of it.

- People have preferred ways for both receiving information and for processing it.

- Large amounts of information can be forgotten very quickly – as much as 40% in five minutes.

Structure

> 'Learning – the most gloriously messy, unstructured, mysterious process known to man.'

John Abbot, President of the 21st Century Learning Initiative

Teaching involves guiding young, immature learners through the learning process. It is a daunting prospect, for learning is undeniably a complex, curious business. It is also highly individual. Not surprisingly, there is no single approach to teaching that will guarantee that students will learn.

Every lesson, students embark on a journey. The fact that they begin their journey from different places, travel at different speeds, in different directions and on different modes of transport presents a considerable challenge for their guide; not least because the system demands that they arrive at the same destination at the appointed time.

The notion of a lesson structure does not deny the complexity of learning; nor does it preclude spontaneity or individuality. It is simply a realistic response to the demands of classroom management. Learning may be individual, but teachers work with groups. Even when we accept that a group is simply a collection of individuals, we do not lessen the challenge.

Teachers have always structured lessons, consciously or otherwise. They have to. The realities of the classroom demand it. Two issues are of particular significance:

1 not *whether* teachers structure lessons but precisely *how* they structure them

2 whether all teachers should adopt a common approach to structuring lessons.

There has been considerable interest in the notion of lesson structure in recent years, the catalyst for this interest stemming from two very different sources:

1 the fact that lesson structure is an aspect of teaching and learning over which teachers have considerable control

2 a growing belief that learning is enhanced when lessons are structured to reflect the way in which the brain learns naturally.

The two sources, although reflecting different motives, need not be contradictory. When we deliberately structure lessons to reflect the learning process, we are likely to improve the quality of learning. When we adopt such a structure as a school policy, we create a management tool that leaders can use to both promote consistency and develop the quality of teaching and learning across the school. It is a potential win–win situation.

When a school adopts a common approach to lesson structure – when it becomes school policy – it becomes a management tool, a lever to exert influence and bring about improvement.

The ways in which the four-phase lesson structure can be used as a management tool are discussed in Section Four, *Leading the improvement process.*

Control and influence

We may not control the mood of the students upon arrival, or their intrinsic motivation and levels of self-belief, but we do have control over the way in which we choose to start our lessons, how long we talk for and what we do in the last ten minutes of the lesson.

Identifying the aspects of teaching and learning over which we have greatest control, and then acting upon them, is a key to improving the quality of learning in a school. This principle applies at two levels, as:

● teachers seek to influence students

● school leaders seek to influence teachers.

There is a strong correlation in the areas where control and influence are greatest, for not only do teachers have considerable control over the way in which they structure their lessons, school leaders also have a high degree of control, or at least influence, in this area.

Just as there are aspects of teaching and learning over which teachers feel they have more control, so there are aspects for which heads find it easier to hold teachers accountable. If a teacher is consistently late for lessons or has failed to mark a set of exercise books for ten weeks, headteachers can act. But when was the last time a head confronted a teacher because she did not smile enough, or because he had failed to congratulate a student as she entered the classroom on her selection for the county squad?

When a school adopts a common approach to lesson structure – when it becomes *school policy* – it becomes a management tool, a lever to exert an influence and bring about improvement. We cannot make people change, but when we state that the school policy is to begin all lessons by sharing learning objectives with students, and by writing them on a whiteboard provided specifically for that purpose in every classroom, it is more likely that they will change their practice accordingly.

Compliance with the policy is easily identifiable and measurable; teachers either filled the whiteboard or they didn't. This is in sharp contrast to judging how effectively teachers motivate and reassure, which involves a significantly higher degree of subjectivity. 'Your introduction lasted for 32 minutes' is a *fact*; 'Your initial questioning strategy put some students on edge' is an *opinion*.

Reflecting the way the brain learns

When we learn, we progress through a series of phases. Even though, as adult learners, we probably do so subconsciously, with considerable blurring of the boundaries, there are nonetheless identifiable, discrete stages of the learning process.

● New learning is built upon the foundations of existing knowledge, the brain finding it easier to understand new detail when it can place it in a wider context. Learning is likely to be more effective, therefore, when the experience is linked to previous understanding and the learner has an overview or big picture prior to receiving detailed information.

Receiving information is not the same as making sense of it. This must be reflected in the way lessons are planned.

- The brain cycles between receiving information and understanding it. In many respects, this is the key to learning, for it is only when we make personal sense of new material that information becomes understanding. It is the 'Ah, I get it!' moment that lies at the very heart of the learning process.

- While understanding something makes it more likely that it will be remembered, it does not guarantee it. There is a real danger that large amounts of information will be forgotten very quickly – some studies suggests that as much as 80 per cent of material can be forgotten within 24 hours. Reviewing information at the end of a learning experience can significantly improve memory.

It has already been acknowledged that learning is a complex, 'gloriously messy' process. However, we are seeking to create a model in an attempt to manage this complexity and, as with any model, this involves deliberately simplifying reality.

Any model of learning would appear to involve four broad phases:

1   placing learning in a wider context

2   receiving information

3   making sense of that information

4   reviewing information.

If the role of the teacher is to help young, immature learners navigate their way through this process, it would suggest that lessons should be based around four broad stages.

Phase one: set the scene; link to prior learning; review previous lesson; provide the big picture; share learning objectives.

Phase two: new information; instruction/exposition; (teaching).

Phase three: processing; making sense of information; understanding; (learning).

Phase four: review.

(A more detailed outline of this four-phase structure, including specific strategies for each phase, can be found in *Strategies for Closing the Learning Gap* – please see page 260.)

WARNING!

Adopting a broad template for structuring lessons does not preclude:

- spontaneity
- creativity
- imagination
- individuality

unless you let it!

The four-phase lesson structure

The four-phase lesson structure is not dramatically different from what most teachers do already – it simply formalizes that practice. It is not designed to be restrictive nor prescriptive – it is a flexible framework, and not a rigid straitjacket. It does not destroy creativity, imagination or spontaneity – unless you let it!

The following points should also be acknowledged.

- Precise interpretation of the four-phase structure will inevitably be very different in different situations. Age, ability, timing of the lesson, subject area and the particular focus for the lesson will all have a significant impact.

- The boundaries between the 'phases' will almost certainly be blurred. For example, in the course of explaining a new concept, a teacher may well ask a series of questions carefully designed to challenge the students to think and so develop their understanding. It is during phase three, however, that the *emphasis* is on developing understanding. By drawing attention to the various facets of learning in this way, we make it more likely that none of them slip through the net.

- Teachers may well scroll through the phases more than once during any lesson. For example, after a short period of exposition, students may be engaged in an activity designed to help them make sense of new material. This may be followed by another period of exposition and an appropriate exercise.

- The phases are not always sequential. Review, for example, is not confined to the end of the lesson. Good teachers weave review through the entire lesson.

- There may be occasions where the template relates more to the overall learning experience rather than an individual lesson. For example, during an extended project or investigation, students may be guided through the discrete phases over a series of lessons.

- The template offers no guarantees; teachers cannot make students learn. However, when lessons are structured to reflect the way in which the brain learns naturally, learning is likely to be enhanced.

- While the structure of the lesson is important, it is the quality of the tasks and activities employed in each of the four phases that will determine how effectively children learn.

- Interpretation is the key. Learning is a complex, unpredictable business. If a lesson structure is allowed to restrict teachers and constrain learners, learning is unlikely to be enhanced and may even be impaired. Great learning has always, and will always, involve spontaneity, creativity and flexibility. The four-phase model is a template, not a straitjacket.

The key to learning is making personal sense of information.

The difference between excellent and satisfactory lessons is often the extent to which students are engaged in their learning and the ways in which they are challenged to think and interact with information.

From both a learning and a teaching perspective, therefore, phase three of the four-phase lesson structure – *understanding* – holds the key.

The biggest single advantage of adopting the four-phase lesson structure is that it emphasizes the centrality of understanding in the learning process and highlights the crucial distinction between teaching and learning.

Effective and manageable

Two things are essential if a common approach to structuring lessons is to improve the quality of learning.

1 Teachers are being asked to guide students through a series of stages. When the bell goes, they are being asked to repeat the procedure with a new group of students. Therefore, the model must be manageable. More significantly, teachers must *feel* that it is manageable.

2 Explicit reference must be made to the fact that teaching and learning are not the same thing. Encountering information is not the same as understanding it. While these stages may be inextricably linked, they are separate processes. This must be reflected in the lesson template.

The four-phase model meets both requirements. The fact that it places *understanding* at the heart of the lesson, both reflects the centrality of understanding in the learning process and focuses attention on the key distinction between information and understanding, teaching and learning.

There is little point to adopting a lesson template if it is not going to improve teaching *and* learning. In both cases, it is phase three that holds the key.

● The difference between an excellent lesson and a satisfactory lesson is often the extent to which students are engaged in their learning and the ways in which they are challenged to think and interact with information.

● Learning is an active process – the product of *doing* rather than *receiving*. For acquiring information is not the same as understanding it and making personal sense of information – understanding it – is what learning is all about.

While high quality exposition in phase two may ensure a 'satisfactory lesson grade', it is unlikely to lead to effective learning unless it is accompanied by the tasks and activities that allow students to digest the material they have been introduced to. In crude terms, while a lesson may be satisfactory when the second phase is done well, it will only be excellent when the second *and* third phases are of high quality.

As school leaders, our key concern is raising the quality of 'satisfactory' (competent, mediocre, 'OK') lessons, so they become high quality learning experiences. From the management perspective too, therefore, it is the third phase that holds the key.

> **Achieving a balance between input and processing, information and understanding, teaching and learning is central to any drive to raise standards. It is a balance that we are more likely to achieve when we make explicit reference to it in the lesson template.**

Phase one
Indicators of excellence

- Teacher creates a relaxed yet purposeful atmosphere.
- Students are engaged without feeling threatened.
- Work from previous lesson(s) is briefly reviewed.
- Lesson is linked to students' prior knowledge.
- Lesson is placed in a wider context – students are provided with an overview.
- Specific learning objectives are shared with students.
- Students know what to look for during the lesson.
- Interest is generated and curiosity stimulated.
- There is a sense of challenge.
- Open questions are asked.
- Problems are posed.
- Targets – collective and individual – are set by the teacher and generated by students.

Phase one – overview

The emphasis in this phase is on:

- creating an appropriate working atmosphere

- linking the lesson to prior knowledge

- providing an overview

- sharing learning objectives with students

- triggering the brain

- stimulating curiosity, generating interest and setting the challenge.

Phase one is the scene-setting phase. Although it is relatively short in duration it includes a number of key features.

Creating an appropriate working atmosphere

Students will not learn if they are not in an appropriate state to learn. In particular, they will not learn when placed under undue negative stress – the ideal state for learning being one of 'relaxed alertness' (page 59). Teachers use a range of strategies to establish a climate conducive to learning, including:

- greeting students at the classroom door

- smiling!

- using first names, enquiring about known interests, and so on

- playing gentle background music

- creating a classroom environment that is reassuring, stimulating and informative

- having an opening activity ready on desks or on the board – students enter the classroom and immediately settle down to work.

Linking the lesson to prior knowledge

Learning involves building on prior knowledge. Not surprisingly, therefore, lessons frequently start by reviewing the previous session. There are many ways that this can be done, one of the most common being a brief question and answer session. While this is a quick and effective way of linking the lesson with prior learning, care must be taken not to place undue pressure on individual students. When this happens, or when students think that it might happen, there is a real danger that students will begin the lesson in a totally inappropriate state to learn effectively.

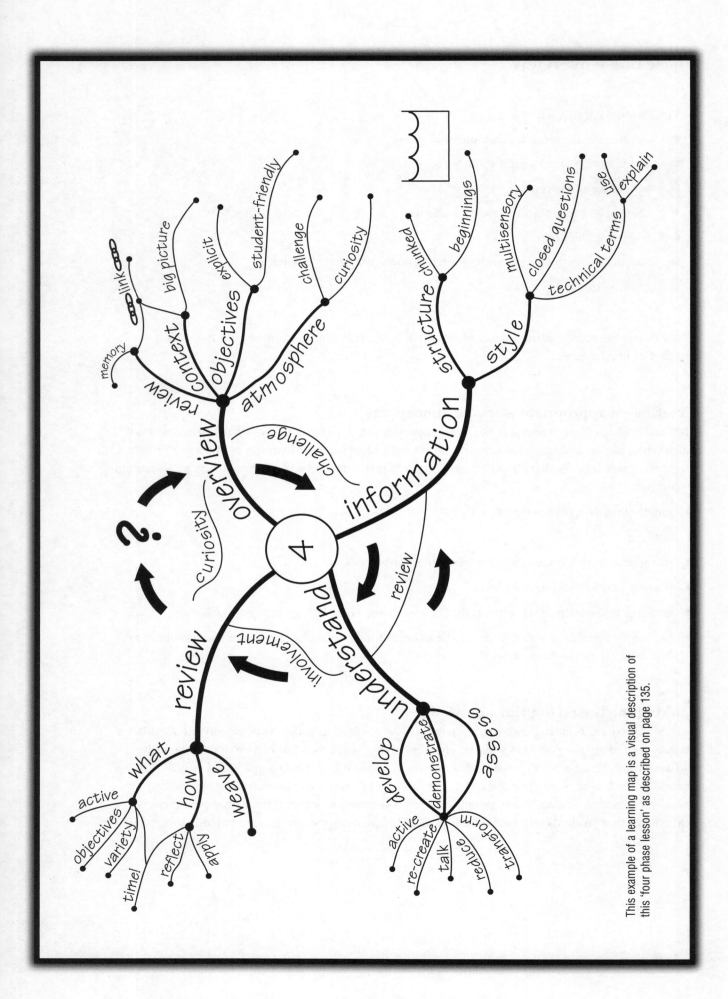

This example of a learning map is a visual description of this 'four phase lesson' as described on page 135.

Other ideas for linking the learning to existing knowledge include the following.

● 'Think of the three most important things that you learned last lesson – now tell the person sitting next to you.'

● 'Alison was away last week – can you tell her the three most important things we learned last lesson?'

● 'I want you to work in groups of four. You have two minutes to identify the three most important things that we did last lesson.'

● 'In two minutes, I am going to ask you what you learned last lesson. Have a think about it. You may look at your books if you wish.'

● 'Today's lesson is about earthquakes. You have two minutes to write down as many things as you can that you already know about earthquakes. You can work in pairs if you wish.'

Providing an overview

The brain is more likely to absorb details when it can place them within a wider context. This is often referred to as 'providing the big picture first'. The analogy often used to illustrate this point is that of a jigsaw: individual pieces will probably mean very little until you have seen the picture on the front of the box, and can see how the parts might fit together to make a meaningful whole.

One of the best ways of providing an overview is to use a learning map (page 96, opposite). Increasingly, teachers are producing giant learning maps for an entire unit of work, so that students have an overview of a series of lessons. These are placed on the classroom wall and referred to at the start of each lesson, enabling students to see how the new information fits into the wider context. A smaller copy of the learning map can be given to the students to keep at the front of their books or files.

An alternative is to provide students with the outline skeleton of a learning map, including just the key words – the equivalent of chapter headings in a book. Students can add their own detail to these personal maps as the lesson progresses, or as a review exercise.

Sharing learning objectives with students

It is not sufficient for teachers to be clear about the learning objectives for the lesson – students must know *exactly* what they are going to learn and what is expected of them by the end of the lesson.

This aspect of the lesson is now being carried out significantly more effectively in a great many classrooms – not least because teachers know that Ofsted Inspectors are explicitly looking for it! For learning objectives to be shared effectively, teachers must:

● move away from saying 'Today we are doing…', and instead say 'By the end of today's lesson you will all know/be able to/understand …'

● make them specific – 'By the end of today's lesson you will be able to do fractions' is too vague to be particularly helpful; instead, be precise and say 'By the end of today's lesson you will be able to convert a decimal into a fraction.'

Stimulating curiosity

- Begin the lesson in an interesting, novel, unexpected way.
- Start by asking an open question or two. Many lessons begin with a flurry of closed questions. It is unlikely that students will be stimulated by too many closed questions.
- Pose a problem to be solved.
- Get students to generate the questions. People will generally pursue an answer to a question that they have generated with more enthusiasm than if the question has been imposed on them. They are also more likely to remember it.
- Set a challenge. 'Your challenge today …' is a different message from 'Today we are doing …' Most teenagers, particularly boys, will respond to the 'I bet you can't' gauntlet.
- Set targets. These can be collective ('Our target today is …') or individual ('Your target today is …').
- Get individuals to generate their own targets. For a target to be effective, it must be specific, individual and related to the learning objectives of the lesson.
- Include a target when marking a piece of work: 'Your target for next lesson is …'

- be positive – 'By the end of today's lesson you will be able to …' immediately establishes high expectations, and is a very different message to 'Today we are doing …' or 'Today I hope you will be able to/some of you will be able to …'

- use student-friendly language – there is little point in sharing learning objectives if students don't understand what you mean

- write them down – while auditory learners may absorb verbal information, many visual and kinesthetic learners won't; many schools are installing a small whiteboard in each classroom for this very purpose, with the permanent prompt 'By the end of today's lessons, you will …'

- refer to them, both during the lesson and during the review phase.

Triggering the brain

The brain will tend to notice things it is has been primed to look for. Thousands of pieces of sensory information bombard the brain every second – if it were to pay attention to all of them, it would quickly go pop! The reticular activating system (RAS) acts as a filter, effectively telling the brain which pieces of information are sufficiently important to demand its conscious attention. The moment that our attention is drawn to something, the RAS is activated and the brain is told, 'This is important – notice it'.

Beginning a lesson by saying 'For homework tonight I am going to ask you to write about three important functions of the liver – you will hear about these functions during today's lesson', or 'During today's lesson you will notice …', triggers the RAS and significantly increases the chances of students absorbing key information when they encounter it.

Stimulating curiosity, generating interest and setting the challenge

When teachers capture the imagination and stimulate curiosity in the first few minutes of the lesson, they go a long way to ensuring a high quality learning experience. On the other hand, when they fail to generate interest and involvement at the start of the lesson, they face something of an uphill struggle for the remainder of the period. Some suggestions are made opposite.

Phase two

Indicators of excellence

- Information is presented in short chunks.

- Exposition is kept brief and does not exceed students' concentration span.

- Teacher frequently asks (closed) questions to check for (shallow) understanding.

- Teacher asks open questions to help students make sense of the information they encounter (phase three).

- Inputs are punctuated by tasks and activities designed to develop understanding (phase three).

- New information is delivered in a variety of ways, to suit students with visual, auditory and kinesthetic learning preferences.

- Teacher uses appropriate technical language.

- Teacher checks that all students understand technical language and subject-specific terms.

Phase two – new information

> **The emphasis in this phase is on:**
> ● providing students with new information.

In crude terms, phase two is the teaching phase. Although we want all students to understand the information as they encounter it, the emphasis during phase two is on *providing* the new information.

New information can be delivered in many ways:

● exposition

● audio–visual aids – video clip, slides, and so on

● textbooks

● graphs, diagrams, pictures, and so on

● ICT – CD-ROM, internet, and so on

● demonstration.

The quality of the input during this phase will have a big bearing upon the extent to which students understand information. While high quality exposition does not guarantee understanding, it does make it significantly more likely. Poor quality teaching in this phase, on the other hand, may not prevent learning taking place but significantly reduces the chances.

A number of techniques can be used to ensure that the quality of input in phase two is kept high.

Keeping periods of exposition short

Students have limited concentration spans. Although much depends on individuals and circumstances, a widely used and useful rule of thumb is that concentration span will be about two minutes in excess of chronological age. Periods of exposition should therefore be kept short and punctuated by regular breaks or activities. In general terms, significantly more learning will take place when new information is transferred and explained in three bursts of around ten minutes than in one 30-minute session.

Creating lots of beginnings

People tend to remember more from the beginning of an experience. This is known as the 'primacy effect'. When exposition or input is chunked into 10–15-minute slots, a number of 'beginnings' are created in the lesson. Punctuate the lesson by giving out resources, collecting in homework or having a two-minute 'timeout', for example. Make the new start obvious. Use phrases such as, 'Now then, we are moving on to a new area' or, 'The next activity is …'

Structuring lessons to exploit the BEM principle

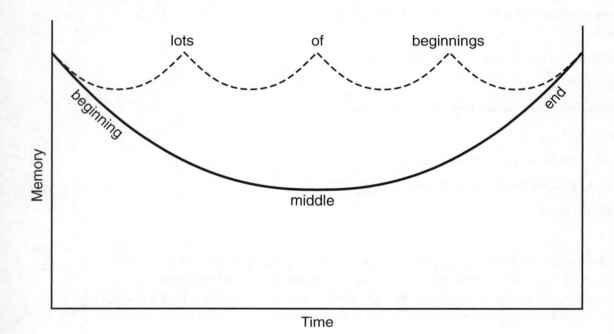

As a rule of thumb, people remember more from the beginning and end of an experience than they do from the middle.

A lesson based around one activity has one beginning, one end and lots of 'middle'.

However, when lessons are 'chunked' into a series of short, sharp activities:

- lots of beginning are created
- activities do not exceed concentration span
- learning is likely to be more effective.

Note

Long activities can be punctuated by short breaks; for example, collect in or set homework in the middle of a 30-minute activity to create two sessions of 15 minutes.

Delivering the key point at the beginning

Most lessons or explanations have a *key point* – the key piece of information or the fundamental rule or principle. A quick way to work out the key point of a lesson is to consider what you would do if the lesson lasted just 60 seconds. Exploit the fact that the brain remembers more from the beginning of an experience – the primacy effect (page 101) – by deliberately delivering the key point at the beginning of the lesson or explanation.

Punctuating the input phase with questions

Although phase two is principally about exposition and delivering new information, it should be punctuated by regular questioning. Different contexts require different techniques – the key is to be clear about why we are asking questions and to ask the appropriate types of questions at the appropriate time. As a general guide:

- ask regular *closed* questions *during* the input. This will keep students alert and provide instant and regular feedback as to whether they have heard correctly and have understood – albeit at a relatively shallow level. Asking too many open questions during an explanation can easily take the lesson off on inappropriate tangents. It also allows an individual to take the lesson off in a direction that causes other students to lose their train of thought. A clear, concise explanation does not need open questions during it – in fact, they can actually detract from the clarity of the input.

- ask *open* questions *before* and/or *after* an input. Posing an open question at the start of an explanation will prime the brain to notice detail and begin to form an answer, even at a subconscious level, during the input. Asking an open question at the end of an input takes the learning into phase three and is designed to develop and assess deeper understanding.

Asking a series of open questions or a combination of open and closed questions as an input, or part of an input, draws to a close is a strategy designed to support students and help shape their thinking. It is interventions of this nature that are often referred to as 'scaffolding' (page 53). This pattern of questioning is effective when phases two and three almost merge into one: as students encounter new information, teachers are simultaneously asking questions designed to help them make sense of it.

Punctuating input with activities

Punctuate the input of new information (phase two) with activities designed to help students make sense of it (phase three). This kind of integrated, alternating pattern of 'phase two, phase three, phase two, phase three' can often be more effective than an extended period of explanation or input followed by a longer period of processing.

High quality exposition does not guarantee understanding – but it does make it more likely.

Delivering new information in several different ways

The fact that people prefer to receive information in different ways (page 69) demands that information is transmitted in more than one way during phase two. A verbal explanation may well be clear, concise and of high quality. However, two-thirds of the class may be working outside of their preferred style and struggling to grasp what is being said.

Most students are sufficiently multisensory to absorb new information, even when it is received outside of their preferred channel – after all, auditory learners can read! However, there are two possible consequences when information is regularly transmitted in just one way.

1   Students will become bored and switch off. Highly visual learners, for example, can easily become frustrated if they are *frequently* required to listen with nothing to look at.

2   Students whose preference for receiving sensory data is particularly pronounced – the 'translators' (page 71) – will almost certainly suffer.

Making learning multisensory

The vast majority of people learn best through multisensory learning experiences; that is, from seeing, hearing *and* doing.

The ideal scenario, therefore, would be that all new information is encountered through a variety of senses. However, the constraints of the classroom and the nature of particular curriculum areas mean that this is not always possible. Often, a compromise position must be sought. For example:

● if each input cannot be made multisensory, emphasize different sensory channels for each new input; that is, if the first input is a verbal explanation, make the second input predominantly visual, and so on

● if information cannot be transmitted in a variety of ways during an individual lesson, make sure that information is presented in a variety of forms during a *series* of lessons.

Explaining technical language

Teachers are often subject experts. As such, it is easy for them to use technical language during periods of exposition, making the erroneous assumption that all the students have understood. Relevant technical language and subject-specific terminology should, of course, be used during phase two – we want to develop and extend students. However, such language should be appropriate to the age and ability of the students and teachers should take care to explain each new word or phrase.

Phase three
Indicators of excellence

- Frequent teacher–student and student–student interactions.
- High proportion of open questions.
- Time allowed for students to think about and discuss their responses to questions.
- Supplementary questions to extend understanding.
- Questions that encourage students to reflect on their thinking.
- Opportunities for students to generate questions.
- Students fully engaged in their learning.
- Tasks that require students to think.
- Tasks that develop understanding.
- Students verbalizing their understanding.
- Opportunities for students to demonstrate their understanding.
- Tasks that enable the teacher to assess understanding.
- Students given opportunities to process information in their preferred style.
- An emphasis on students *re-creating* rather than reproducing information.

Phase three – processing

The emphasis in phase three is on:

● developing understanding

● demonstrating understanding

● assessing understanding.

This is the key phase. It is the opportunity for students to make sense of information; the time when the penny drops, the light comes on and students silently exclaim, 'Ah, I get it!'.

Not surprisingly, it is often the quality of the third phase that distinguishes 'excellent' from 'satisfactory' lessons.

Developing understanding

Although understanding is personal, students do not work alone. Teachers play a significant role during this crucial third phase, encouraging and reassuring at an emotional level and guiding, prompting and challenging on a cerebral plane. In particular, teachers engage students during phase three through both learning tasks and interactions (page 55). In many respects, it is the quality of these tasks and interactions that determines the extent to which information will be understood.

There are no guarantees – teachers cannot *make* students understand – but they can significantly increase the chances of its happening by engaging the learner in a meaningful way. More specifically, the extent to which students will understand information depends on four factors, all features of excellence in the third phase.

1 Quality of interactions

It is teachers who help students make sense of information. The frequency and nature of interactions between teacher and students is therefore highly significant. Developing understanding requires that teachers:

● ask a large proportion of open questions

● allow sufficient processing time for students to think about their answers before further intervention

● allow students to talk to each other

● ask supplementary or extension questions to extend understanding

● ask questions to encourage students to reflect upon their thinking

● *challenge* thinking – play 'devil's advocate'

● help students re-frame experiences by prompting, paraphrasing and reflecting.

(A checklist of effective questioning strategies can be found on page 108.)

Effective questioning strategies

1   Use open questions. ('Effective teachers have been found to ask more open questions than less effective teachers' – Daniel Muijs and David Reynolds*.)

2   Provide wait time – students need time to think through their answers before replying. (According to Muijs and Reynolds, 'For open-ended, higher-level questions a longer wait time [up to 15 seconds] is required'.*)

3   Provide thinking time by giving an advance warning, such as 'In two minutes I am going to ask you …', or 'At the end of the lesson I am going to ask you …'

4   Allow students to explore and articulate their thinking by giving them two minutes to discuss their response in pairs or groups. Group responses are reassuring – it is easier to say 'Our group think …' or 'We think …' than it is to say 'I think …'

5   Ensure students fully understand the question by asking them to re-word it for someone three years younger than they are.

6   Extend and deepen thinking by asking follow-up question(s) to the same student.

7   Help students to think about their thinking by asking follow-up questions such as 'What made you think that?'

8   Students often give the first answer that comes into their heads without really thinking it through. Ask students to identify three possible answers and then select the best one.

9   Provide, or get the students to generate, ten possible answers by 'snowballing'. ('Think of three reasons; now work in pairs to see if you can get five; now work as a group of six and get eight … now select the best answer.')

10   Scaffold thinking and answering – for example:

● 'In two minutes I'm going to ask you X, but before I do, I'd like you to think of (or talk about) A. Now I'd like you to think about B. Finally, I'd like you to think about C. Now, how do you respond to the original question (X)?'

● 'In two minutes I'm going to ask you X. Normally I would ask you to consider three things before answering. Which three things do you think I'll highlight on this occasion?'

How frequently do I/we use/observe each of the strategies above?

1 = frequently   2 = sometimes   3 = rarely   4 = never

(* Please see recommended reading list on page 260)

2   *Frequency of opportunities for students to generate questions*

Students are required to answer a large number of questions – the majority of questions in the classroom are teacher-generated – yet *asking* questions is fundamental to learning. Learners ask questions to clarify, probe and extend their understanding.

Often, students are reluctant to ask questions during lessons, afraid of making fools of themselves. The onus is therefore on the teacher to both create frequent opportunities for students to ask questions and reduce the perceived risk of ridicule.

This can be achieved by, for example:

● encouraging pair- or group-generated questions – 'Our group …' or 'We …' is easier to say than 'I …'

● the teacher working with small groups

● using question boxes, or question walls – students can generate and 'post' questions anonymously

● the teacher using prompts such as 'Normally, I would ask a question now. Can you think what I might ask?'

3   *Talking*

There is an old saying, 'If you want to know a subject, teach it'. As with so many such sayings, there is much sense to it. When we talk, we do more than articulate our current level of understanding. The very act of talking forces us to organize our thoughts – a kind of subconscious processing – and so deepens understanding. It is partly the reason why we remember so much of what we teach – famous research suggests that we remember as much as 90 per cent of what we teach, compared to around 5–10 per cent of what we read and hear.

There are many who would suggest that talking about information and articulating your thinking is a key to developing understanding. Among the most notable is Win Wenger, Director of Project Renaissance, who argues that 'what you express is 10 to 100 times more productive of your learning than what is expressed to you'.

Talking about the work in which students are engaged can take many forms. For example:

● students could explain something to a teacher

● students could explain something to a partner or a group

● talking could be formal – students carry out a piece of research and report back to the rest of the class, individually or in groups

● talking could be informal – 'Sanjay was away last lesson; can you tell him the three most important things that we learned?'

● peer coaching

● students could be asked to explain the work to someone who is two years younger – simplifying in this way further develops understanding.

Scaffolding thinking and answering

● Do I understand the question?

● Have I thought about it?

● Have I talked about it?

● Have I come up with more than one possible answer and selected the best?

● Do I have evidence to justify my answer or an example to illustrate it?

● Have I said my answer aloud or in my head to see if it 'sounded right'?

● Have I tested my answer – asked myself what's wrong with it?

● Does my response answer the question?

Provide students with a checklist such as the one above of things to consider before giving their answer to a question. Enlarge it, laminate it and display it on the classroom wall. Use it to teach students how to answer questions – for example, emphasize the importance of considering more than one possible answer – and to remind them of the steps they need to go through when considering their response.

4   Tasks that engage students and challenge them to think

Making personal sense of information involves re-creating and assimilating it into existing understanding. It is an active process and demands that the learner actually *does* something, not least at a cognitive level. Tasks in the crucial third phase should:

- require students to do something at a cognitive level

- provide a degree of challenge

- require students to *re-create* rather than *reproduce* information

- develop understanding

- allow students to demonstrate their understanding

- give the teacher an opportunity to assess understanding.

Two of the most effective and useful strategies for phase three, which generate tasks that meet the above criteria, are reduction and transformation.

- **Reduction**:

    When students are required to reduce information, they are challenged to think. For whether the task is to rank order, summarize or prioritize – reduction comes in many guises – it requires some significant decisions. Reduction tasks include the following.

    1   'Summarize in 100 words …'

    2   'Rank order the following statements …'

    3   'Which event was the key turning point in … the Second World War/Cinderella/ the discovery of the structure of DNA?'

    4   'Which is the most important sentence/paragraph/chapter?'

    5   'Who is the most important character in the story?'

    6   'What is the most important section of the diagram?'

    7   'Underline the six key words.'

- **Transformation**:

    However information is presented to students, ask them to change it. Transforming information in this way requires the student to re-create meaning – a process fundamental to understanding. Transformation tasks include the following.

    1   'Convert this text into a labelled diagram/flow chart/cartoon strip/picture.'

    2   'Describe this graph/diagram/photograph/model in your own words.'

    3   'Put the keywords of this topic to music' or 'Use the keywords in a poem.'

    4   'Portray this piece of text/diagram as a mime/frieze/play.'

    Transformation, while being an effective learning activity in its own right, is also an easy way of accommodating different types of learner in the classroom (page 83).

(Further strategies for phase three are outlined in *Strategies for Closing the Learning Gap*, pages 195–219.)

Apply the understanding test

- How is this activity helping students to *understand* the information?

- Is the emphasis on reproducing or *re-creating* information?

- How does this activity allow students to *demonstrate* their understanding?

- How does this activity enable the teacher to *assess understanding*?

Demonstrating and assessing understanding

While the focus of phase three is *developing* understanding, teachers also have to *assess* the extent to which an individual student has grasped a new concept or new information. This is difficult, if not impossible, when the task has primarily involved reproducing information. It is equally difficult if the evidence is no more than a successfully completed but low-level comprehension exercise that has required the student to do little more than search a piece of text for the relevant clues (page 53).

If teachers are to assess understanding, the tasks students are given must allow them to *demonstrate* their understanding. Although there is rarely one correct answer, the way in which a student reduces or transforms information, for example, provides some important clues as to their level of understanding. Similarly, the quickest and one of the most effective ways of judging a student's level of understanding is to listen to him or her explaining something.

There are two key questions to be considered at the end of phase three.

1   What have the students understood?

2   How do you know?

Beware, therefore, of:

● students writing down things they don't understand

● copious note-taking

● low-level comprehension exercises (page 53)

● students copying graphs, diagrams, and so on

● using a large proportion of closed questions

● activities that lack challenge – colouring, cut-and-paste tasks, and so on

● *students reproducing rather than re-creating information.*

In order to focus attention upon aspects of teaching and learning, include subheadings for each lesson in your teachers' planner. These could be based upon the four key phases of the lesson, or include prompts such as, 'How will *learning* be assessed?'

Subheadings of this kind – which could be printed in a grey tint rather than in solid black, to avoid cluttering the layout of the planner – will act as a constant reminder for teachers when planning lessons.

Thanks to Cheshunt School, Hertfordshire, for sharing this strategy.

Phase four
Indicators of excellence

- Sufficient time devoted to reviewing *what* has been learned.

- Students actively engaged in the review process.

- Explicit reference to learning objectives.

- Students encouraged to reflect on *how* they have learned.

- Information provided in order to stimulate thought before the next lesson.

Phase four – review

The emphasis in this phase is on:

- reviewing what has been learned
- reflecting on how it has been learned.

Review is a key to memory and certainly not confined to the end of the lesson. Good teachers weave review throughout the entire lesson and are constantly referring students back to the objectives of the lesson, and reinforcing prior learning. Reviewing material is a highly significant part of the learning process, not least because large amounts of information can be forgotten very quickly. The brain is not designed to remember content, and research by Ebbinghaus conducted in the late eighteenth century suggests that as much as 40 per cent can be forgotten within five minutes (page 116)!

Phase four is the time when review takes centre stage and becomes the main focus. It is also, however, the phase of the lesson that is so often neglected as teachers run out of time in the closing minutes of the lesson.

Key features of phase four are described below.

Active involvement of students

One of the key reasons why we forget is a failure to pay conscious attention to something for long enough. In a sense, we forget because we do not choose to remember. When the teacher ends a lesson by summarizing what has been learned, the effect on the students' memories will therefore be relatively insignificant. However, when the *students themselves* identify what they have learned as the lesson draws to a close, their memories will be given a significant boost.

Use prompts such as:

- 'What are the three most important/interesting things you've learned today?'

- 'What three questions could you answer now that you couldn't answer at the beginning of the lesson?'

- 'Imagine you have a brother a year younger than you who asks you what you learned in history today – what would you tell him?'

Although it is important that the students identify what they consider to be the most important message from the lesson, the teacher can provide some guidance. As the students reflect on the lesson, the teacher could quietly say something like 'You may be thinking that the most important thing was …'!

The Ebbinghaus curve of forgetting

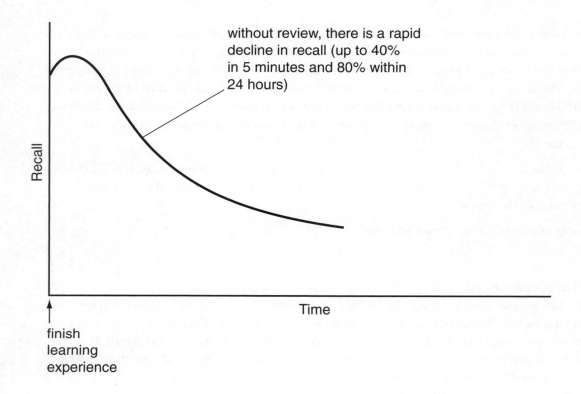

without review, there is a rapid decline in recall (up to 40% in 5 minutes and 80% within 24 hours)

Recall

Time

finish
learning
experience

The brain is not designed to remember large amounts of content. Famous research conducted by the German Ebbinghaus in the late eighteenth century suggests that

- up to 40% of material can be forgotten within five minutes

- up to 80% of material can be forgotten within 24 hours.

Teachers employ a range of strategies, including using mnemonics, to help students remember information. One of the most effective strategies is to review information at the end of the lesson. Reviewing information strengthens and effectively prolongs the memory.

(For further information, see *Strategies for Closing the Learning Gap,* pages 220–227.)

Referring to the learning objectives

Now is the time to refer to the learning objectives written up at the start of the lesson. For example, if the objective as the lesson began was for students to know X, that is precisely how the lesson should end. Students should leave the classroom knowing what they know, and the best way for them to do this is to demonstrate, explain or do the thing in question.

Students reflecting on what they have learned

Teaching involves more than explaining content. Teachers seek to develop the skills and attitudes necessary for young people to develop into confident and successful independent learners. Reflecting upon how they tackled a particular task, what they would do differently next time and how the learning methodology could be applied in a different context, is a key to their development as autonomous learners.

Reflection of this kind need not be time-consuming or onerous. Try these prompts.

- 'How did you tackle the problem/go about the task?'

- 'What were the advantages of working in this way?'

- 'Were there any drawbacks with the way in which you chose to work?'

- 'What alternative ways of approaching the exercise can you think of?'

- 'What would have been the advantages/disadvantages of these alternative ways of working?'

- 'If you had to do a similar task again, how would you approach it?'

- 'If you had to give one piece of advice to someone tackling the same task tomorrow, what would it be?'

- 'What did you do today that you found most helpful when you were learning?'

- 'What did you do today that you found less helpful?'

Never finishing a lesson with a full stop – always a question mark

Prime their brains by telling students what they will be learning next lesson. When this is presented as a question, problem or riddle, there is a chance that students will begin to think about the issue and try to answer the question – even at a subconscious level – during the time before that lesson.

Informing students what they will be doing in the following lesson activates the reticular activating system (page 99) and essentially tells the brain to notice something. For example, having been told that the next lesson is all about how birds fly, when students next see a bird flying they will both notice and think about the event differently.

Ending with a smile

Lessons should end where they began – with a smile. There should be a clear message sent from teacher to students that 'I enjoyed that and I'm looking forward to teaching you next lesson'.

Every lesson, students embark on a journey. The fact that they begin their journey from different places, travel at different speeds, in different directions and on different modes of transport presents a considerable challenge for their guide – not least because the system demands that they all arrive at the same destination at the appointed time.

Summary

1 Teaching is not the same thing as learning.

2 State, style and structure are the keys to effective learning.

3 People learn best when they are in an appropriate physical and emotional state. Learning is optimized when the brain is nourished and students are relaxed, confident and motivated.

4 Teachers do not control levels of motivation and self-belief. However, we do influence them. We are more likely to be effective when we do so consciously, consistently and congruently.

5 People learn best when they are given frequent opportunities to work in their preferred style.

6 An individual learning style is a complex combination of how people prefer to receive information, how they prefer to process information and the ways in which they are intelligent.

7 The key to accommodating different learning styles is variety and choice. Variety and choice do not just happen, however – they have to be planned for.

8 Learning involves understanding. Making personal sense of information is central to learning.

9 Lesson activities must therefore be designed to develop understanding, allow students to demonstrate their understanding and give teachers opportunities to assess understanding.

10 Learning is enhanced when lessons are structured to reflect the way in which the brain learns naturally.

11 Adopting such a lesson structure provides school leaders with an effective management tool for improving the quality of teaching and learning.

INSET is an *event*; improvement is a *process*.

An event needs to be staged; a process needs to be led and managed.

Section Four

Leading the improvement process

The specific aims of this Section are to:

■ challenge school leaders to reflect upon the way in which they currently manage the quality of teaching and learning

■ suggest a framework and a range of specific strategies that have proved effective in improving the teaching and learning in a variety of schools

■ help school leaders identify the bit they can tweak to increase the chances that teachers will tweak.

Widespread improvements rarely happen by chance – people generally require a catalyst to prise them from the comfort zone. Improving the quality of teaching is a managed process and it is the responsibility of headteachers and school leaders to initiate, drive and manage it.

This, of course, is often easier said than done. We cannot *make* people change – we can only create the conditions that will make it more likely that teachers will be prepared to step out of the comfort zone and develop their practice. Not surprisingly, there is no single correct approach. However, we are more likely to be successful when our management strategy is based upon the following principles.

● Improving the quality of teaching is a managed process that requires both challenge and support.

● Change is unlikely to be successful if teachers feel that it will significantly add to their workload.

● Change is more likely to be successful if teachers feel that they have a creative role in the process.

● People are more likely to tweak – make small but significant adjustments to their practice – than to transform.

● Successful change takes time.

How effective are you at improving teaching and learning?

This exercise can be completed by the leadership team, middle managers or the entire staff.

Work in small groups. How effective is the school at *improving* teaching and learning, currently? Award a mark out of ten (ten being the top mark) for each of the following areas.

(1) How effective is our current in-service training programme? ☐

(2) How good are we at embedding ideas from in-service training (INSET days, coaching, courses, and so on) into classroom practice? ☐

(3) How effectively do we share good practice *within* departments? ☐

(4) How effectively do we share good practice *between* departments? ☐

(5) How effective is our current observation programme? ☐

(6) To what extent does observation lead to improvements in classroom practice? ☐

Of particular significance are:

● areas that receive a wide range of marks – what is the cause for this disagreement?

● areas that receive low marks from most or all groups – we are seeking to identify the areas that would most benefit from a tweak.

Where are you now?

Improving teaching involves influencing people and creating conditions that increase the likelihood that they will change and develop their practice. When we develop our leadership expertise in this area, we increase our influence and enhance the prospect of teachers improving. In other words, *we have to tweak our leadership styles and structures to make it more likely that they will tweak their teaching.*

How effective are you as a headteacher, or as a leadership team, at *improving* the quality of teaching throughout the school? Award yourself a mark out of ten.

- **What evidence have you used when awarding your mark?**

- **Some headteachers or leadership teams would score one mark higher than you. What do they do that you don't?**

- **What is stopping you from scoring one mark higher?**

- **What one thing could you do differently that would enable you to raise your score by one mark?**

Whatever mark you awarded yourself, you will remain at this level until you find something to do differently. It doesn't have to be dramatically different – a tweak will suffice – but *it must be different.*

Key factors

The success of any attempt to improve the quality of teaching in a school is largely dependent upon three key factors:

1   people

2   time

3   a framework for improvement.

All three are necessary to substantially improve the quality of teaching. You cannot perm two from three – even the most charismatic, persuasive leader will struggle to make an impact if weighed down by conflicting tasks and priorities. Similarly, creating time for energetic leaders will not guarantee success – charisma must be accompanied by a coherent and realistic strategy.

Where are we now?

Staff perception questionnaire

Respond to each question with an answer
from list A *and* list B.

List A	**List B**
1 frequently/strongly agree	1 very important
2 sometimes/broadly agree	2 reasonably important
3 occasionally/broadly disagree	3 not very important
4 rarely/strongly disagree	4 not at all important

	List A	List B
(1) There is a clear emphasis upon teaching and learning in this school.	☐	☐
(2) Staff development is a priority.	☐	☐
(3) INSET days are used effectively.	☐	☐
(4) INSET days are followed up with further discussion/activities.	☐	☐
(5) INSET days lead to changes in classroom practice.	☐	☐
(6) Teachers are encouraged to try out new ideas in the classroom.	☐	☐
(7) Support is readily available for teachers wishing to try out new ideas in the classroom.	☐	☐
(8) Lesson observations are helpful.	☐	☐
(9) Teaching and learning appears on the agenda for departmental meetings.	☐	☐
(10) Good ideas for lessons are shared between teachers within department/between departments.	☐	☐

People

It is people who bring about change. The personal qualities of the key change agents are therefore critical. Substantial improvements to the quality of teaching in a school are rarely brought about by leaders who lack energy, determination, commitment and enthusiasm.

Leaders too have to be prepared and able to both challenge and support. Crucially, they must be able to instinctively gauge the appropriate balance between the two and judge when to change the emphasis. Not least, they have to be persuasive – it is difficult to influence on a wide scale unless you are influential.

Many of these qualities are inherent and heavily dependent upon *personality*. Headteachers cannot fundamentally alter the personalities of their senior staff; this is something largely beyond their control. It means that the way in which they deploy senior staff is an important factor in managing improvement. Round holes require round pegs.

Ultimately, improving teaching and learning requires an ability to influence. It is essentially an intangible quality that defies description and while we can equip people with a range of strategies to enhance their effectiveness, the ability to influence is a gift that we cannot bestow. Yet, we all instinctively recognize people who are naturally persuasive. The fact that we do not always know why they are influential is not important – knowing who they are is sufficient. These are the people who we need to manage the improvement process.

> **Who is your most persuasive, influential senior member of staff?**
>
> **What role does he or she play in improving the quality of teaching in the school?**

Senior or middle managers?

In many schools, a member of the senior leadership team is responsible for managing the quality of teaching and learning. Some schools, however, adopt a totally different approach and invite a member of the middle management team to chair a teaching and learning group. Both approaches have potential strengths and weaknesses.

While a senior member of staff is likely to be both an experienced manager and an effective teacher with considerable managerial 'clout', teachers can easily feel, even subconsciously, that someone of such seniority is a threat. Whatever the personal qualities of the individual concerned, however sensitively they manage, it is essentially a hierarchical model and if it is perceived as an accountability exercise it is understandable that teachers might be a little defensive.

- Is the person in charge of teaching and learning also the person responsible for continuing professional development?
- If not, why not? If improving teaching isn't about professional development, what *is* it about?

- Who has overall responsibility for teaching and learning in your school? Who leads the teaching and learning group?
- Is this person a member of the senior leadership team?
- What subtle messages are conveyed by selecting this particular person to take responsibility for developing classroom practice?
- Does it suggest that the focus upon teaching and learning in your school is essentially about accountability or about professional development?

- Consider the likely impact of inviting people who do not feel that they are anything other than unexceptional to join or even lead a teaching and learning group.
- To what extent would the 'I value you and your work' messages make it more likely that some of the teachers in the middle ground would adopt new approaches and develop their practice? (The enthusiasts will be doing it anyway!)

The situation is reversed when a member of staff from outside the senior leadership team has responsibility for developing teaching and learning. While the sense of threat is reduced, a teacher lacking both actual and moral seniority may lack the managerial muscle to make a difference. What you gain in support and reassurance you lose in challenge.

Much depends on context: when the situation calls for greater challenge, someone who is capable of cracking the whip is required; when a softer approach is called for, someone who is perceived as less of a threat may be more effective at encouraging reluctant colleagues to try out a new idea. It's 'horses for courses'.

A further alternative is to combine the best features of both approaches – a member of staff from outside the senior leadership team chairs a teaching and learning working party, to give a clear message that the initiative is about growth and development rather than accountability, while a member of the senior leadership team acts as line manager or mentor to provide the challenge or managerial guidance as necessary.

Involve or isolate?

Who is asked to join a teaching and learning working party or research group? Even more significantly, who is asked to lead it – the inspirational, successful and enthusiastic teacher, or the cynic? How many working groups consist of volunteers – people who are essentially keen to see developments taking place in the classroom?

'Going for winners' in this way is a widespread and understandable approach to promoting innovation in the classroom as we seek to generate a momentum and win over a critical mass of staff. There is indeed a certain logic to this approach. However, there is a real danger that a number of teachers – often the cynics or the competent but unexceptional – will be, or at least will feel, isolated from the process. Recognition and being made to feel special are basic human desires. It is unlikely that people excluded from a working group will have those desires satisfied. On the contrary, there is an implicit message in the 'go for winners' approach – a message received, if not intentionally sent – that the work of those outside of the group is not valued.

Taking a line-of-least-resistance approach is designed to avoid the cynic, at least in the initial stages. However, it can all too easily backfire. Exclusion can *fuel* cynicism. It is human nature to want to belong. If teachers do not belong with the enthusiastic innovators, they may well decide, often at a subconscious level, to belong with the sceptics. At an extreme level, some people will seek solace in their cynicism, wearing it almost as a badge of honour and a visible sign of belonging.

An early and inevitable casualty in a situation like this is perspective. There is no middle ground – you're either in or out, one or the other. Reality is distorted as perceptions and opinions are increasingly polarized, the status quo and traditional methods – whatever they may be – being equated with standards and discipline. The more enthusiastically the innovators pursue their goal, the more doggedly the cynics defend their position and resist change. It is a response that satisfies nature's innate search for balance.

How much leadership time is spent on the 'urgent but not important'?

	Urgent	Not urgent
Important	1	2
Not important	3	4

Things that are 'not important', in this context, are those that do not contribute to long-term, strategic improvement.

- How much time do you personally spend in each of the four quadrants?

- How much time does each member of the leadership team spend in each of the four quadrants?

- How much time does the leadership team collectively spend in each of the four quadrants?

- How much time does the person with overall responsibility for improving teaching and learning spend in each of the four quadrants?

The matrix was developed by Stephen Covey*, who suggests that leaders of high performing organizations manage to spend between 65 and 80% of their time on the 'important but not urgent' (quadrant two) and as little as 15% of their time on the 'urgent but not important' issues (quadrant three).

This contrasts sharply with leaders of less successful organizations who Covey suggests spend as much as 60% of their time on 'urgent but not important' issues and only 15% of their time dealing with the 'important but not urgent'.

The key is the balance between urgent and important issues. It is the difference between management and leadership, improvement and maintenance.

(* *First Things First* by Stephen R. Covey – see recommended reading on page 260)

Time

Teaching and learning is, for the vast majority of schools, high on the list of priorities. Indeed, for many schools it is top of the list. However, this level of priority is not always reflected in the amount of time and energy devoted to it. Yet time is a key ingredient. Without it, even the most talented manager and inspirational leader will struggle to make a difference.

- **How much of a priority is improving teaching and learning for your school? Award a mark out of ten (ten being the top mark).**

- **How much time, effort, energy and emotion do you personally put into improving teaching and learning in your school? Again, award a mark out of ten.**

- **How would the rest of the senior leadership team respond to the two questions above?**

- **To what extent does the amount of time, energy and emotion devoted to improving the quality of teaching reflect its importance?**

Urgent or important

- When a desire to improve teaching and learning is not matched by a considerable commitment to this aim, it is highly unlikely that much will change. A significant discrepancy between your marks out of ten for *priority* and for *time* (the first two questions in the box above) is therefore of interest. Is improving the quality of teaching *really* a high priority?

- Schools that are successful at managing the quality of teaching and learning do not have more time than others. They just choose to spend it differently. Consider the grid on the page opposite. How much management and leadership time is spent in your school upon things that are 'urgent but not important'? ('Not important' in this context relates to issues that do not contribute to long-term improvement.)

- The success of an institution is often the difference between the amount of time spent in quadrant three – 'urgent but not important' – and that spent in quadrant two – 'important but not urgent'. Quadrants one and four take care of themselves. Rightly, all organizations spend a considerable amount of time dealing with the issues that are both urgent and important. Not surprisingly, little time is devoted to those things that are neither urgent nor important.

- Many of the 'urgent but not important' issues are task-related. Tasks are urgent because they have deadlines – cover for Tuesday has to be done by Tuesday, the Wednesday newsletter has to written by Wednesday. In order to meet the deadline, less urgent issues – such as a lesson observation – inevitably make way. *In the struggle between tasks and improvement, tasks inevitably come out on top.*

'The main thing is to keep the main thing the main thing.'

Stephen R. Covey

- Some 'urgent but not important' issues, such as dealing with irate parents or incidents of poor behaviour, are not only time-consuming but emotionally draining, and steadily erode the energy levels of the leader. Thus the leader's efficacy at managing improvement in teaching and learning is diluted by conflicting pressures and priorities.

- The challenge is clearly to spend more leadership time on the 'important but not urgent'. However, this is easier said than done – despite the best of intentions, when all senior staff have a combination of task and improvement responsibilities, there is a real danger that tasks will deflect *all* members of the team from the important improvement issues.

- Improving teaching demands a considerable time commitment. For just one teacher to make one lasting change to their practice may require an initial chat, a planning session, a lesson observation, support in the classroom when they first try the new strategy out, followed by a debriefing session. Not all teachers require this level of support, of course, but for some it is intervention of this nature that is the crucial difference between a strategy being tried in the classroom and remaining just another good idea.

- The levels of intervention and support required to improve teaching suggest – in an ideal world, at least – that the improvement of teaching and learning should be given to someone as their *sole responsibility*. For if this key person is also required to manage a range of other issues, such as arranging cover or running the school diary, the chances of him or her having the necessary time and flexibility to make a substantial, widespread difference to the quality of teaching are remote.

What would be the impact of a senior member of staff claiming the improvement of teaching as his or her only priority, and devoting all of his or her professional time, effort and emotion in pursuing this aim?

Almost certainly, it would increase the chances of changes actually taking place to improve the quality of teaching in the school.

- While it may be ideal for one person to have the improvement of teaching and learning as his or her sole responsibility, it is not always realistic particularly for a primary or small secondary school. In many schools, senior leaders have to wear many hats. The challenge for school leaders, then, is to get as close as possible to this ideal management structure. Although there is no single answer – all schools operate in unique contexts – a possible way forward is to consider the balance of task and improvement responsibilities held by each member of the senior leadership team.

Leadership team structure

Reflect upon the current roles and responsibilities of members of your senior leadership team.

In what ways does this structure *help* your efforts to improve the quality of teaching throughout the school?

In what ways does this structure *hinder* your efforts to improve the quality of teaching throughout the school?

Is there a tweak you can make to the structure of the leadership team that will make it more likely that your efforts to improve teaching and learning are successful?

Consider the person who has overall responsibility for the quality of teaching in
your school. Is improving teaching and learning:

- **his or her sole responsibility?**
- **his or her prime responsibility?**
- **just one of his or her responsibilities?**

What distracts this person from developing the quality of teaching?

More time in quadrant two

While the challenge is to spend more leadership time on important improvement issues, this does
not mean that *all* senior staff should spend the majority of time in the 'not urgent but important'
sector in the grid on page 128. It does, however, demand that *collectively* more time is spent in
quadrant two at the expense of quadrant three.

By removing, or at least reducing, the *task-related* responsibilities of the teacher responsible for
teaching and learning, we effectively deploy that person in quadrant two. We may not be able to
afford to ask him or her to concentrate on improving teaching for 100 per cent of the time – he or
she will almost certainly have to assume responsibility for other areas as well. However, by
dramatically reducing the deadline-driven, 'urgent but not important' aspects of that person's
folio, we significantly increase the chances that he or she will have sufficient time – not to
mention energy, emotion and flexibility – to make a difference.

> 'Anything less than a conscious commitment to the important is an
> unconscious commitment to the unimportant.'

Stephen R. Covey

Even the most charismatic, energetic and determined leader needs a coherent strategic plan.

A framework for improvement

Even the most charismatic leaders need a plan. Improving the quality of teaching across a school is a complex and lengthy process and requires a strategic framework. Schools will, of course, already have a strategic plan in place to improve the quality of teaching. This section aims to:

● prompt schools to reflect upon the effectiveness of their current procedures

● offer a framework for improving teaching.

Two discrete models are outlined in this section.

The four-phase lesson	The DIIR model
1 overview	1 diagnosis
2 input	2 input
3 processing	3 implementation
4 review	4 review

The models do not have to be adopted wholesale. All schools operate in unique circumstances and are at different stages of development. These models are no more than loose templates and schools can implement individual aspects of either framework to dovetail with and compliment existing policies.

They are stand-alone models. However, there is huge overlap between the two and they are arguably most effective when used in conjunction.

These models are based around the notion of tweaking (pages 43–46). Tweaking involves making small but significant adjustments to current practice and therefore requires both precise diagnosis of the bit to tweak and specific strategies to make the tweak.

Identifying the bit to tweak

This can be done individually or collectively.

Reflect upon each of the phases of the four-phase lesson structure (pages 91–117).

● Award yourself a mark out of ten for how effectively you teach each phase.

● Which phase do you teach relatively most effectively?

● Which phase would benefit most from a tweak?

● Identify one strategy in each phase that you could introduce into your lessons to enable you to improve your mark out of ten for that phase by one point.

Phase	Mark out of ten	Strategy to be introduced
One – overview		
Two – input		
Three – process		
Four – review		

Using the four-phase model

The four-phase lesson offers a generic framework and generates a common language within a school that can provide both clarity and impetus to any improvement programme (for example, see Section Seven, *Case studies*, page 227). It is more than a template for planning lessons – it is a management tool, a lever for school leaders to use in their drive to improve the quality of teaching and learning.

The four-phase model can be used for a variety of purposes: by individual teachers as a template for planning, teaching and self-evaluation, or by school leaders as a framework for monitoring, observation and structuring an improvement programme. Whichever way it is used, the major benefit of such a model is that it focuses attention upon *aspects* of the teaching and learning process and thus provides the precision required for teachers to successfully tweak their practice.

Identifying the bit to tweak

> **Using the four-phase lesson model, award yourself a mark out of ten for your effectiveness in carrying out each of the four phases. This activity can be done informally, by discussion or as a piece of focused research. It can be done by senior managers, middle managers or all members of staff. It is equally effective when applied to an individual teacher, to a curriculum area or to the whole school.**

Irrespective of whether you awarded yourself high marks or relatively low marks, it is highly unlikely that the same mark was awarded for each phase. We all have relative strengths and weaknesses.

Many teachers, for example, acknowledge that they frequently omit a substantial and meaningful review of what has been learned as the lesson draws to a close. This is not because they are unaware of the importance of reviewing material, fundamentally object to the practice or feel that a plenary session takes them out of their comfort zone. They simply forget – the summary gets squeezed out as the clock ticks down.

Tweaking simply involves drawing attention to the specific parts of the lesson that would benefit from a bit of polish. As such, it is both specific and reassuring. 'We need to remember to spend the last few minutes of a lesson reviewing what we have just learned' is a very different message to, 'We need to improve teaching and learning'.

The difference between satisfactory and excellent

For each of the four phases of the lesson:

- identify the differences between 'satisfactory' and 'excellent'
- identify the key indicators of excellence.

(Indicators of excellence can be found in Section Three, *What do we know about learning?*)

Phase one – overview

Phase two – input (new information)

Phase three – processing (making sense)

Phase four – review

Adding layers

It is possible to tweak teaching and learning still further by adding some 'layers' to the basic model. This involves being even more specific and precise in the diagnosis of the bit to tweak and recognizes that, although all learners need to receive and make sense of information in order to learn, they will do so in very different ways (pages 69–74). 'Adding layers' in this way enables us to enhance even high quality teaching as we move from asking 'How effectively are we teaching and helping students learn?' to 'How effectively are we teaching and helping *individual* students to learn?'

On a scale of one to ten, how effectively do you:

- teach each phase of the lesson?
- teach each phase to:
  1 visual learners
  2 auditory learners
  3 kinesthetic learners?
- Teach students who:
  1 process logically and sequentially
  2 process randomly and intuitively?
- give students opportunities to learn through their dominant intelligence?

Understanding the learning process

Teachers rarely complain that they have too much time to reflect upon what they do for a living – namely, help children learn. Yet regular professional reflection – 'Why do we do what we do?' – can only be beneficial, not least because people are more likely to make a change when they accept that there is a need, particularly when they do not have to do so publicly. Use the four-phase model as a basis for discussion and reflection.

- **Although all four phases of the lesson are important, which do you think is the most significant?**

  (There is, of course, no right answer, but this can provoke considerable debate.)

- **Alternatively, make a case for each of the four phases in turn as – identify two factors to support the argument that phase one is the most significant, then do the same for phase two, phase three and phase four.**

From satisfactory to excellent

Just because teachers base their lessons around four phases, this does not guarantee high quality learning. It is the specific strategies employed and how well the phases are carried out that will determine how effectively students learn. All teachers therefore need to be clear about the difference between satisfactory and excellent in each of the four phases. This kind of clarification exercise is a worthwhile activity in its own right (page 138, opposite).

Time

The length of time that teachers spend in the various phases of the four-phase lesson structure offers an indication of whether the emphasis is on teaching or on learning. Is time being spent transferring information or is time being devoted to helping students make sense of it?

● How long do you *think* that you spend in each of the four phases? Pay particular attention to the proportion of time spent in phases two and three.

● How long do you *really* spend in each phase?

What teachers think they do and what they actually do are often quite different things.

It is easy for teachers to spend a longer time in phase two than:

● they think they do

● they would like to

● phase three.

The four-phase model as a management tool

There are two keys areas that we can focus attention upon as we manage the improvement process:

1   the length of time that teachers spend in the various phases

2   what teachers actually do in each phase (strategies).

Time

The amount of time teachers spend in the various phases of the lesson offers an indication of whether the emphasis is on teaching or on learning. Is time being spent transferring information or is time being devoted to helping children make sense of it?

A multitude of factors will, of course, influence the precise length of time spent in each phase during a particular lesson. However, when we analyse how long an individual teacher spends in the various phases over a period of a few weeks, patterns invariably emerge. Often they reveal significant differences between curriculum areas; sometimes they reveal noticeable differences between teachers in the same department.

Teachers almost universally spend longer in phase two than they think they do, and in many cases longer than they would wish. Although there is usually significant variation across the curriculum, many teachers in secondary schools spend considerably longer in phase two (teaching) than they do in phase three (helping students learn).

A number of factors draw teachers to phase two like a magnet.

1   **They are good at it**: teachers are subject experts and almost universally good 'on their feet'. Phase two is the teacher's 'bread and butter'.

2   **Behaviour**: most teachers, if only at a subconscious level, feel that it is easier to manage behaviour while they are in phase two. Many teachers equate phase three with relinquishing control to the students.

3   **Curriculum coverage**: teachers face the daunting challenge of covering a large amount of content in a relative short period of time. The problem is particularly acute in certain subject areas. Phase two is an efficient way of getting through content quickly.

Yet, when phase three is neglected – for whatever reason – lessons are reduced to little more than the transfer of information. Focusing attention upon, and tweaking, the amount of time that teachers spend on the various aspects of the lesson – particularly the balance of time spent in phases two and three – can generate significant improvements to the quality of learning.

Disseminating good practice

- How much meeting time is devoted to administration, policy-making, and so on, compared with time spent swapping good ideas for the classroom?

- What is the mechanism for teachers to disseminate good practice – that is, swap good ideas?

- Do departmental meetings include teaching and learning, in the form of 'Good ideas for the classroom', on every agenda?

  Do all departments do this?

  Is it a requirement?

- Is there a mechanism for teachers to swap good ideas *between* curriculum areas?

- Are strategies and activities for classroom practice included in schemes of work, or collated in the form of a staff or departmental handbook?

How effectively do teachers share good ideas within your school? Award a mark out of ten. What could you do to increase this score by one mark?

Note

Many teachers are wary of the phrase 'disseminating good practice', as they perceive it as carrying an implied criticism of their own practice. 'Swapping good ideas' is an effective alternative.

Strategies

Guiding students through the four key phases of the learning process does not guarantee learning. It is the quality of the strategies adopted in each of the phases that largely determines how effectively students learn.

In particular, it is the strategies that teachers consciously employ in the crucial third phase of the lesson that is the key to students understanding the information they have encountered. Generating and swapping strategies that engage students, and challenge them to think in greater depth about information, can lead to some significant tweaks being made that can tilt the balance from simply covering material to really learning it.

However, the factors that draw teachers to phase two cannot be dismissed. They are significant, not least because teachers *think* they are. This means that the specific strategies that we suggest for the crucial third phase have to take these concerns into account. They cannot take too long, nor can they significantly increase the risk of poor behaviour. If they do, teachers – even if they acknowledge their value as learning activities – are unlikely to adopt them.

The strategies of reduction and transformation outlined on page 111 take these genuine concerns into account. Asking students to identify the six key words in a paragraph or convert a piece of text into a labelled diagram:

- does not take an excessively long time

- does not run a high risk of poor behaviour

- can be done individually and in silence, or collaboratively.

However individual teachers interpret these strategies, they are still effective at developing understanding. The fact that they do not run a particularly high risk of poor behaviour is reassuring for many teachers, and significantly increases the chances of their being adopted in the classroom.

All schools have excellent teachers. More specifically, all schools have members of staff who excel at particular aspects of teaching. They will be employing a range of strategies, which could easily be adopted by all teachers. Often, these strategies do not require teachers to leave their comfort zones and do something significantly different. We are just looking to extend the range of strategies at teachers' disposal – movement *along* rather than *out of* the comfort zone (page 18).

Collect good ideas for each of the four phases of the lesson.

- **Identify strategies that you, as an individual, currently employ.**

- **Extend this process – share ideas within curriculum areas.**

- **Share strategies *between* curriculum areas – often techniques become synonymous with particular subjects, yet, with a bit of adaptation, can be effective generic learning strategies.**

One step at a time

Focus upon each lesson phase in turn for a period of time. During this period:

- focus all lesson observations exclusively (or at least primarily) on the appropriate phase

- ensure that there are no conflicting priorities or initiatives

- use departmental meetings to generate and share good ideas for use in the relevant phase – these can then be written into schemes of work, or collated in some form of staff or departmental handbook

- provide subject-specific, tightly focused training or coaching (Section Five, *Coaching*)

- support teachers as they introduce strategies into their lessons for the first time (pages 193 and 195)

- go slowly – writing ideas into schemes of work, preparing materials and embedding a strategy into daily classroom practice *takes time.*

A possible schedule for development

Begin by focusing attention on **phase one** for a fixed period – about half a term. In particular, concentrate upon sharing learning objectives with students at the beginning of the lesson. Installing a small whiteboard in each classroom with the permanent prompt 'By the end of today's lesson, you will all be able to …' will make it more likely that teachers will start lessons by outlining what students will be able to do by the end.

Extend the idea of sharing learning objectives at the beginning of a lesson into providing the big picture at the beginning of a unit, module, key stage or exam course. This can provide an opportunity for providing training in, and encouraging teachers to use, learning maps in the classroom. Learning maps are one of the most effective ways of providing students with an overall framework or big picture. They can be used in the classroom in a variety of ways and are being used increasingly on classroom walls to provide students with the framework of a larger unit of work. (For more details, see page 261.)

Switch attention to **phase four** for a period of six weeks or so. Again, make this the sole focus of attention during this period. A meaningful plenary is often omitted from lessons because teachers forget, or run out of time, or lack effective strategies to use when summarizing the work.

Simply drawing attention to the importance of reviewing work helps. (Some schools are ringing a ten-minute warning bell before the end of the lesson to remind teachers to begin the review!) However, we must also spend time generating and sharing good ideas for ending lessons and reviewing information. There are no guarantees, but we are looking to make it *more* likely that *more* teachers on *more* occasions will end their lesson with a substantial review of what has been learned. (Ideas for ending lessons can be found on page 117.)

By initially focusing attention upon phases one and four, two things will hopefully happen.

1   A considerable tweak will be given to the quality of teaching and learning by tightening what is happening during the crucial first and last ten minutes of lessons.

2   By focusing attention on the least contentious areas first, a momentum can be generated and a sense of progress created, that will make it easier to tweak phases two and three.

It is, however, the quality of the strategies employed in the crucial third phase, and the proportion of time spent in phases two and three, that is often the difference between a good and an excellent lesson and will determine the extent to which students understand what they have been taught.

Adopting the four-phase model

It has been proposed that you adopt the four-phase model across your school to provide a focus for improving teaching and learning.

Consider your response to this proposal. Use Edward de Bono's 'six hats' to structure your thinking (a very useful thinking tool for staff meetings!).

This activity can be carried out individually, or as a collective exercise.

Six hats – a framework for thinking

Edward de Bono

Red hat   emotions, intuition, feelings, hunches, no need to justify feelings, 'how do I feel about this right now?'

Yellow hat   positive thoughts, good points, why it can be done, how it will benefit us

Black hat   negative thoughts, bad points, weaknesses, caution, what's wrong with it

Green hat   creativity, different and new ideas, suggestions, alternatives, variations

White hat   information – what information do we have, what other information do we need and where can we get it?

Blue hat   thinking about thinking – what have we done so far, and what do we need to do next?

Phase three is the key phase. The aim is to both:

● develop and extend the range of strategies available to teachers

● encourage teachers to use these strategies on a regular basis.

We are more likely to be successful when we:

● **focus upon one specific strategy in turn**. For example, begin by focusing on the strategy of 'reduction' (page 111). Put a subject-specific slant on the technique and look for opportunities in schemes of work to use the strategy. Translate the generic principle into concrete lesson activities. Concentrating upon a single strategy is a realistic way of approaching change. Teachers are not required to make dramatic, wholesale adjustments, just incorporate one specific activity into their lessons.

● **support teachers** (pages 193 and 195) as they try out the strategy for the first time. Spend as long as is necessary for teachers to become comfortable using it and only move on to a second strategy – for example, 'transformation' (page 111) – when the original technique has been successfully introduced and embedded in practice.

● **adopt a collective approach to generating and implementing strategies**. By focusing upon and evaluating strategies rather than people, we de-personalize the issue. 'That strategy that *we* developed didn't seem to go as well as we hoped it would' is a very different message from '*You* taught a lousy lesson'. The mutual support and reassurance of working collaboratively and collectively makes it more likely that teachers will be prepared to try out new ideas and venture out of the comfort zone.

● **link developments to existing and new initiatives**. For example, the emphasis of the national Key Stage 3 strategy is on engaging students in their learning in a meaningful way. There are aspects of the strategy – such as developing thinking skills, teacher intervention and questioning techniques – that directly relate to phase three.

How would *you* respond to the proposal that your school should adopt the four-phase lesson structure to provide a focus for improving teaching across the school? Use Edward de Bono's 'six hats' – outlined on page 146 opposite – to structure your thinking.

● **Spend three minutes 'wearing' each hat in turn. Be strict. For example, when you are wearing a yellow hat, do not allow yourself to say, 'ah, but ...'**

● **Spend five or ten minutes summarizing (reducing!) your thinking. For example, summarize your overwhelming emotional response to the proposal. Crystallize your positive thoughts, and then your negative thoughts, and so on.**

A framework for improving teaching

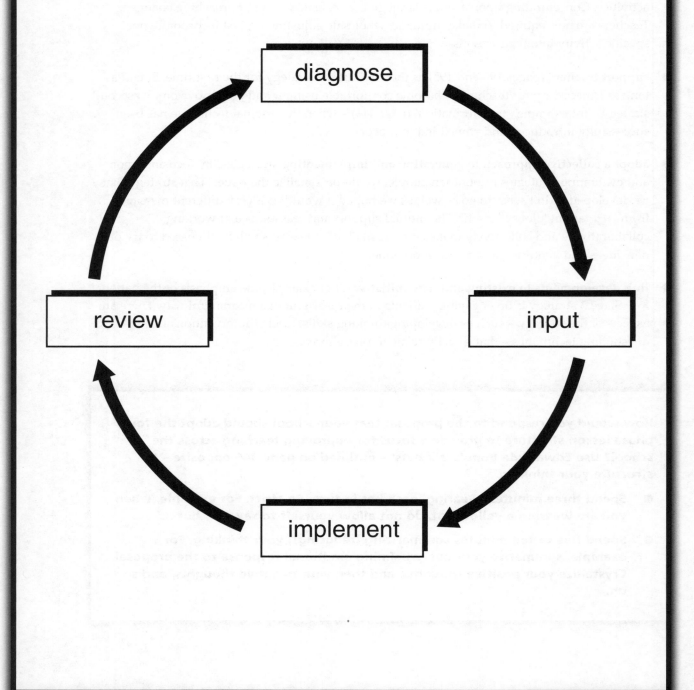

Using the DIIR Model

The DIIR model is a four-phase model for classroom improvement.

1   Diagnostic phase – identifying *what* to tweak

2   Input phase – identifying *how* to tweak it

3   Implementation phase – tweaking it

4   Review phase – Are we tweaking? Are the tweaks making a difference?

The DIIR model:

● is based on the principle that all four stages are necessary to improve the quality of teaching. When we neglect any of these distinct and discrete phases, we significantly reduce the likelihood that training will be effective and result in significant and sustained improvement.

● works on a range of scales. Improving the quality of teaching in a school involves improving individual teachers. DIIR can operate at an individual, department or school level. DIIR can form the basis for individual coaching, which is discussed in more detail in Section Five.

Phase one – diagnosis

The key to phase one is the *precise diagnosis* of the bit to tweak. 'Improving teaching and learning' is too vague; so too is 'Turning satisfactory lessons into good ones'. We need to be much more specific.

Phase one is unlikely to be effective when:

● observation/reflection is insufficiently specific

● observation/reflection fails to focus upon *aspects* of lessons, or of teaching and learning

● observation/reflection concentrates on teaching rather than learning

● data generated by observation is not used for evaluation and diagnosis.

Observation

- What happens to the data generated by the lesson observations that take place in your school?

- To what extent are lesson observations used for monitoring?

- To what extent are lesson observations used for evaluation and diagnosis?

- How specific is the data generated by lesson observations?

- Do you involve students in this process?

- Do your criteria for lesson observations focus upon teaching or learning?

- How much observation training do you provide?

- How often do you co-observe lessons in order to calibrate judgements?

- On a scale of 1–10, how effectively do you currently diagnose the bit to tweak?

- What is one thing you could do to raise your score by one mark?

Key issues

- Precise diagnosis is a prerequisite for tweaking. Aiming to 'improve teaching' is far too vague. We must be clear about *precisely* which aspects of current practice require attention in order to bring about an improvement.

- This is particularly true when teaching is already good. Competent practitioners in any field require relatively minor, but highly specific, adjustments to their practice in order take a step forward.

- Pinpointing the bit to tweak can be done *by* or *for* people. Individuals can diagnose their own strengths and weaknesses through a procedure of reflection and self-evaluation. Most people, however, require some form of catalyst before they engage in such a process. Alternatively, diagnoses can be done by a coach, mentor or manager – usually as part of a lesson observation and feedback programme.

- People are more likely to embrace change when they accept the need. In reality, therefore, it is often a combination of internal reflection, prompted by the external stimulus of a lesson observation that holds the key to improving practice.

- Teachers can learn much from watching their colleagues in action and, while observing a fellow professional at work, can often identify strategies and techniques that would benefit their own teaching. However, although teachers instinctively recognize good practice when they see it, if they cannot pinpoint precisely why it is so effective, they are unlikely to apply it in their own classroom.

- Lesson observation is a key tool in diagnosing strengths and weaknesses of teaching. However, it can be a blunt instrument if the process lacks precision.

Feedback, coaching and, therefore, improvement are heavily dependent upon the quality of the observation programme.

People are more likely to see something when they are looking for it. This means that the quality of observation is heavily dependent upon the quality of the observation *criteria*.

Using the Ofsted criteria

Schools would be foolish to ignore the Ofsted criteria for judging the quality of teaching. Not only do they comprise a comprehensive and generally well regarded checklist, they are also the criteria that schools and teachers will be evaluated against during formal inspections.

However, for the purposes of internal observation, it should be noted that:

- the Ofsted criteria are externally generated – there is no staff ownership of, or involvement in, their development

- the criteria are insufficiently specific. For example, 'Use methods which enable all students to learn effectively' is open to considerable interpretation. What methods are they? How will we know them when we see them?

- although the Ofsted framework makes explicit that teaching is to be judged in terms of its impact on learning, many of the criteria focus primarily on teaching rather than learning.

The Ofsted criteria are therefore best used as a basis for further discussion – a foundation for schools to base their teaching and learning policy and observation checklist upon.

A suggested approach

1   Divide the staff into groups of about four to six teachers.

2   Allocate each group two of the Ofsted criteria – there will be some duplication in large schools.

3   For each criterion, teachers should identify ten *observable indicators* – things you can see, hear or ask – that will indicate that good practice is taking place.

4   A senior member of staff should collate the responses as a draft for further discussion and development.

Within a very short space of time, a checklist for observation can be produced, which:

- is based on the Ofsted criteria

- has been generated by the entire staff

- is specific

- focuses on learning.

Observation

How effective is your current observation procedure?

How specific are your criteria for lesson observation?

Criteria for excellent lessons, and observation checklists, frequently outline *what* teachers should be doing, but rarely make explicit *how* they should go about it.

For example, one criterion for good practice might be that 'Teachers should engage students and challenge them to think'. Few would disagree with this statement, and yet, because it doesn't outline precisely *how* teachers can engage and challenge students, it is less likely that:

1   teachers will be able to do it

2   observers will be able to notice it when they see it happening in the classroom.

Teachers are largely left to their own devices when trying to address the criteria, and observers are dependent upon their subjective judgement when evaluating the extent to which the criteria have been met.

Effective checklists, and teaching and learning policies, include explicit *observable indicators*. These are the things that you can see, hear or ask that will tell you that a criterion is being met and that good practice is taking place. An easy way of doing this is by adding the 'how' to the 'what', as in the example in the table below. It is a crucial, but often neglected, second step in generating lesson criteria.

Step one – 'what'	Step two – 'how'
'Teachers should engage students and challenge them to think.'	'They do this by: ● asking open questions ● challenging students to reduce information ● inviting students to transform information ● encouraging students to explain their thinking.'

Do your observation criteria focus on teaching or learning?

The purpose of all lesson observations, be they part of an internal process or of a full-blown Ofsted inspection, is to evaluate the way in which teaching impacts upon students' learning. What progress have students made during the lesson? What do they now know and understand as a result of this lesson? What can they do now that they could not do before this lesson?

However, when observation criteria focus upon teaching rather than learning there is a real danger that many of the criteria can be met without learning taking place. For example, teachers may have excellent subject knowledge, be well prepared, have excellent visual aids, maintain the pace of the lesson and keep students on task. However, if children don't get to the 'Ah, I get it!' moment, then they haven't learned anything.

Calibrating observation

If two observers observed the same lesson, would they see the same things and make the same judgements?

How do you know?

Try a simple calibration training exercise.

- Identify someone (preferably an Ofsted-trained Inspector) who can work with your team of key observers (for example, heads of department).

- Agree the criteria by which lessons are to be evaluated. (Either use your lesson observation checklist or the Ofsted criteria.)

- Show a video of a lesson. Observers evaluate the lesson and discuss their judgements. Make sure that everyone understands the observation criteria.

- The trainer then co-observes a lesson with each member of the team of key observers in turn. (Make sure that the teacher being observed is comfortable having two observers present.)

- Each observer feeds back to the trainer. What did he or she see? How did he or she judge the lesson?

- The trainer and observer discuss their observations and calibrate their judgements, before the observer provides feedback to the teacher who was observed.

- The exercise provides a clear indication of how accurately and consistently observers are judging lessons.

Note

It is easy for an observer to 'over grade' a lesson. Although we are evaluating the teaching rather than the teacher, we cannot divorce personalities from the process. When relationships are good, it is easy for an observer to judge a close colleague sympathetically and give him or her 'the benefit of the doubt', if only subconsciously. Although understandable, this does little to help the improvement process.

While it is unlikely that learning will take place if teachers are not well prepared, do not have excellent subject knowledge and do not keep students on task, preparation, organization and competent *teaching* will not necessarily lead to high quality *learning*. In simplistic terms, the criteria that emphasize teaching evaluate how effectively teachers explain and transfer information and yet the key to learning, and the difference between satisfactory and excellent lessons, is the extent to which students *understand* that information.

People will tend to see what they are looking for. This would therefore suggest that, if *learning* is to be the focus of our attention, observation criteria should be based upon learning, or at least make explicit reference to it. The indicators of excellence for phase three on page 106 could form the basis for an observation checklist. For example:

- 'How are students engaged in their learning?'

- 'How is this activity helping students develop and demonstrate their understanding?'

- 'Is the emphasis on reproducing or re-creating information?'

- 'What is the proportion of open and closed questions?'

- 'What proportion of the lesson is spent on phase three activities?'

Who generated the observation criteria?

Lesson observations, even in the most supportive of schools, carry a degree of threat and discomfort for many people. However pure the motive for observation, teachers' practice is still the subject of evaluation. When a senior member of staff or a small working party develop the observation criteria and procedure in isolation, the process can easily carry the subtle message that it is essentially about monitoring and accountability. Observation is being done to people.

Teachers are more likely to change when they feel part of the process. Lesson observation criteria can – and indeed should – therefore be generated by the entire staff. This needn't take long – much can be achieved in a couple of staff meetings. There are a number of advantages of adopting this approach.

1   It is a worthwhile development activity in its own right.

2   Teachers feel part of the process.

3   The criteria can focus on learning rather than teaching.

4   The criteria can be specific and address the 'how' as well as the 'what'.

Do you observe lessons, or aspects of teaching and learning?

When people observe a lesson, they often leave the classroom with an *impression* of what they have seen. While this may be sufficient for general monitoring, it often lacks the precision necessary for specific diagnoses. This is particularly true when the observer lacks experience and/or the teaching being observed is of high quality.

The difference between 'good' and 'excellent' is sometimes difficult to detect. Often, it is the 'micro factors' – small, subtle, yet highly significant variations in the precise nature and timing of teacher intervention, or in the quality of questioning, for example – rather than the more obvious 'macro factors', such as lesson structure and content, that make the crucial difference.

Observation – the golden rules

1   Watch the students more than the teacher – otherwise there is a danger that the teaching rather than the learning becomes the focus of the observation.

2   When recording observations, begin sentences with the phrase 'the students …' This further helps to focus attention on learning.

3   Continue recordings using the word 'because'. This turns attention to the teaching and allows the observer to consider what impact the teaching is having upon learning – that is, what the students do as a result of what the teacher does.

4   Link teaching, learning and behaviour. What is the impact of each on the others?

5   Watch the lesson, not the checklist – many experienced Ofsted Inspectors do not write for a third or more of the lesson.

6   Focus on what you see – rather than what you expected to see, usually see, didn't see, and so on.

7   Concentrate upon the impact of the teaching on learning – not on the way *you* would have taught the lesson, or would ideally like to see the lesson taught.

8   Ask yourself two questions.

   ● What have they learned?

   ● How do you know?

The precision and depth of detail required for observations of this nature demand that aspects of teaching are isolated and put under the microscope. Lesson observations – at least some of them – therefore require a specific focus. For example, if the focus of the observation was 'questioning technique', the observer may be considering some or all of the questions below. They are more than enough for a single observation!

● What is the balance of teacher-generated and student-generated questions?

● What is the balance of open and closed questions?

● What is the pattern of questioning? Does the lesson begin with an open question or a flurry of closed questions?

● What is the gender split? How many questions are addressed to boys and to girls?

● How long does the teacher allow for students to answer questions before intervening?

● Does the teacher allow time for thinking or discussion before requiring an answer? (For example, does the teacher use expressions such as 'You have two minutes to think about your answer to the following question', or 'You may discuss your response with the person sitting next to you.')

● Does the teacher ask follow-up questions to the same student to challenge and extend his or her thinking?

● Does the teacher ask questions that require students to justify their thinking or explain how they arrived at a particular answer?

How much observation training do you provide?

If observation is ineffective, the chance of precise, diagnostic feedback and subsequent tweaking is remote. Observation is the starting point of the entire process, yet how much training do schools give to observers? Many schools are investing large amounts of money into observation programmes. It is only money well spent if it leads to improvements in the classroom.

Occasionally, the weak spots of a lesson are glaringly obvious. In these circumstances, observation is a relatively straightforward business. However, the differences between 'highly competent' and 'excellent' are often subtle, small and difficult to spot. While a specific checklist may help inexperienced observers look for the pertinent issues, it will not guarantee that they will see them.

There are two main reasons for providing observation training.

1   There is little point in establishing a comprehensive observation programme if lessons that are no more than satisfactory are consistently being over graded (that is, judged as being of higher quality than is actually the case).

2   When teaching is already of a high quality, there is reduced scope for improvement. Only a highly skilled observer is able to detect the minute aspects of an overall excellent lesson that could be improved still further.

Impact of INSET or training	Probable/possible reasons
(A) Poor training experience – no impact. Possibly hardens negative feelings towards INSET.	• Poor trainer • Diagnostic phase (page 149) neglected – training therefore fails to address pertinent issues, or is not context-specific • Absence of tight brief for trainer with explicit intended outcomes
(B) A few enthusiasts try things. Majority of staff unaffected. However, enthusiasm wanes, momentum is lost and things revert to the status quo – due to poor initial experiences, feelings of isolation, and so on. Little or no sustained, significant change.	• Lack of (perceived) support and encouragement • Small numbers of enthusiasts work in isolation – lack of mutual support • Lack of support from immediate line manager – often HoD • Competing initiatives and priorities
(C) Enthusiasts try things. Working group established. Working group consists of volunteers, positive staff, possibly including a rep from each department. Attempts to disseminate good practice. Some developments in enthusiasts' classrooms. Often good teachers and good lessons become very good and excellent. However, majority of staff remain unaffected – no significant change in majority of lessons. Satisfactory lessons remain so.	• Initial support for enthusiasts and working group • Attempts to disseminate developments and encourage others to make changes are ad hoc • HoDs resist changes proposed by members of their departments who are part of the working group • Confusion of status of working group • There is no *requirement* to act • Teachers who are not part of the working group begin to feel resentful • Developments are not *managed* by senior member of staff • Conflicting initiatives and priorities divert time, energy and enthusiasm • Working group members eventually become dispirited
(table continued on page 160)	

Phase two – input

Having identified the bit to tweak, we need to consider *how* to tweak it. This may well involve some kind of input in the form of training or coaching.

> **The key to this phase is translating the areas we need to work on into specific strategies that teachers can implement in the classroom.**

This phase is unlikely to be effective, however, when:

- phase one (diagnosis) is neglected and training is too general, covers too large an area or fails to address the key issues

- training fails to generate practical strategies that teachers can use in the classroom

- we fail to provide the time necessary to write materials and produce new resources.

Training

> - **How effective is your current training programme?**
> - **To what extent does training bring about improvements in classroom practice?**

Training comes in a variety or forms. While there is a growing emphasis on coaching (Section Five), the staff development or INSET day remains a major form of training input.

INSET can be entertaining or otherwise, high quality or not. However, the bottom line position is the lasting difference that an INSET activity makes in the classroom. Thousands of pounds are spent annually on courses and conferences, speakers and books. Is it money well spent?

Sadly, all too often, INSET fails to bring about the desired changes in the classroom. Although there will be exceptions – there are usually a handful of enthusiasts who will give anything a go – there will be some, often a majority of teachers, who remain relatively unaffected by the training. If we can identify why this is so, we can begin to plan INSET experiences that will make it more likely that teachers will implement aspects of the training in their classroom.

> **Some potential INSET scenarios (A–E) are outlined on pages 158 and 160, with some possible reasons why the changes failed to take hold. To what extent are they familiar?**

Impact of INSET or training	Probable/possible reasons
(D) Enthusiasts try things. Working group established consisting of volunteers. Some other teachers gradually come on board. Increasing numbers of staff involved in developments as enthusiasts 'infect' new staff. As a 'critical mass' is established (in departments or across the school), developments gain momentum. Significant developments in some classrooms. Some developments in significant number of classrooms. No or little development in small number of classrooms.	• Successful expansion due either to energy and personal qualities of enthusiasts and/or to systematic approach to 'infection' as part of a managed programme • Development is sole priority • Staff given time to develop materials and support in implementing them • Opportunities created for dissemination of good practice, observation, and so on • Success of project keeps enthusiasts enthusiastic and a momentum is established and maintained
(E) All staff involved in planned, managed response to training event. Enthusiasts implement most of training with enthusiasm. Other staff implement some of training with little or no enthusiasm. A few staff implement as little as possible but still moan about it! Significant change in some classrooms. Some change in most classrooms. Small amount of change in all classrooms.	• Planned, managed process • Training or INSET part of ongoing improvement loop, involving all staff • Leadership of headteacher and senior team • Middle managers involved in managing programme in subject area • Sole priority • Time provided to produce materials and write into schemes of work • Support provided during implementation phase • Focus for departmental meetings and ongoing training • Focus for observation and feedback • Appropriate balance between challenge and support

The difference between the outcomes in the various scenarios described on pages 158 and 160 is very often down to leadership and management, and the extent to which training is seen as part of a process. For INSET is an event; improvement is a process. While an event needs to be staged, a process needs to be led and managed. Whether or not training leads to improvement is heavily dependent upon the follow-up activities and the way in which the implementation phase (phase three, page 175) is managed. However, any effective improvement programme still requires high quality input.

There are five key requirements of training

1 *Training must be specific*

Tweaking requires specific training to address the specific issues identified during the diagnostic phase. Many schools hold INSET days on teaching and learning, yet how many INSET days are devoted to specific *aspects* of teaching, such as starting lessons, questioning techniques, motivation, phase three activities, and so on?

Off-the-peg training sessions, however interesting and enjoyable, run the risk of failing to address the particular issue that is important for a particular school at a particular moment in time. All schools operate in unique circumstances and are at different stages of development. Training experiences must take this into account and be context-specific. Trainers, therefore, however skilled and credible, need to be provided with a tight brief for the training session with training outcomes made explicit. They also need to be clear about the particular circumstances of the school and the previous developmental work that has taken place.

2 *Training must include an opportunity for reflection*

People are more likely to change when they want to and accept the need for it. Reflection and self-evaluation activities should therefore be built in to all types of professional training. Reflection does not just involve thinking about something, however; often the key to meaningful reflection is thinking about something *in a different way*. Therefore the process requires a catalyst – something to challenge the prevailing wisdom and probe current thinking. Training and trainers can provide such a stimulus.

Managed discussion groups are among the most effective contexts for reflection activities, for it is through professional dialogue and debate that perceptions are challenged, ideas shaped and connections made. Even when teachers emerge from a discussion with their opinion intact, the process of explaining and justifying that view to colleagues can only be beneficial, as articulating a view helps people to understand it more fully.

However, discussion groups can all too easily end up talking about the status quo – it is not unknown for teachers to spend time in discussion groups talking about why a new strategy wouldn't work in their classroom. We all have thousands of thoughts every day of our lives – sadly, they are often the same ones! When we talk to the people we regularly talk to about the things we often talk about, the chances of having a conversation that we have already had – many times – is very high.

If INSET days fail to generate concrete strategies, it is highly unlikely they will lead to significant improvements in the classroom.

Discussions like these are unlikely to lead to people changing practice. For practice to change, teachers have to think about the same things differently. They are professionals; they do not simply need to be told what to do. However, they are also people and, as such, occasionally need to be challenged – without being threatened – to look at things through different eyes and hear things through different ears.

3 Training must generate concrete strategies

Teachers may or may not be interested in learning theories and the latest research. What they really need are concrete strategies that they can implement in the classroom. Training must generate concrete lesson strategies, for improvements will not take place when teachers are unsure of what a concept – however plausible and compelling – 'looks like' in the classroom. Training must therefore provide either ready-made strategies or at least clear direction for teachers to develop the ideas themselves.

4 Training must include a subject-specific dimension

Although there are generic issues – all teachers are primarily involved in learning – the demands of teaching PE, a foreign language, mathematics or science, are very different and therefore require specialist input. Generic training has a place but must, at some stage, be supported by subject-specific training.

5 Time must be made available to produce resources

Time must be made available for writing materials and producing resources. It is naive to assume that all teachers will be so enthused by the training that they will go away and find time in their already busy schedules to prepare new activities. Even when the training has been well received and generated some good ideas, they will often remain good ideas unless teachers are nudged into action. Teachers do not necessarily require large amounts of time to prepare materials, but they do need some. To generate the time required, you could, for example:

- hold INSET *mornings*, and devote the afternoons to translating the ideas introduced during the morning into material for lessons

- take INSET days in pairs, and devote day one to training, reflection, discussion, and so on and the second day to preparing resources

- devote all scheduled meeting time for the three weeks following an INSET day to follow-up writing activities

- allocate to each department one supply day after each INSET day – they can then decide how best to use this time to produce teaching resources.

Time alone, however, will not ensure that teachers produce lesson material. It is easy for departmental time during INSET days to degenerate into general discussion. Time has to be provided for a specific purpose and at the end of the session teachers or departments *must be held accountable*. If time has been provided for a teacher or department to produce a resource, at the end of the time period, someone – possibly a line manager – wants to see it.

Support options

Support and training are available from a range of sources. Considering your options is a helpful exercise. These can then be displayed in the form of a matrix, with sources of support as column headings and types of support as row headings.

A possible options matrix is shown on page 166.

Sources of support

The column headings of the matrix might be:

- on-site
- off-site

Schools may prefer three headings:

- on-site
- cluster-based
- elsewhere

Or different configurations to reflect circumstances:

- school-provided
- EAZ-provided
- LEA-provided
- specialist college network-provided
- other providers

The sources of support available to schools will vary with circumstances, but whatever range of sources is adopted, it is important to include school-based approaches for the reasons given on page 165.

Types of support

Types of support available might include, for example:

- defining standards of practice
- exposure to good practice
- preparatory training
- coaching/mentoring
- sharing good practice/developing networks.

Sources of support

Support and training are available to schools from a range of sources. Knowing the options is a helpful exercise – a suggested approach is offered opposite.

Although a range of training inputs is available, the key decision to make is whether training should come from an internal or external provider. There is of course no single correct answer; different circumstances and situations will require a different approach. However, it is worth bearing in mind the following points.

Internal sources

Schools often seek training from external providers when the necessary expertise already exists on the staff. In general terms, the further from the school the support is located, the greater potential for the approach to be generalized rather than context-specific. Internal, or at least local, solutions to internal problems are often the most effective.

- Input and support is managed or delivered by people who understand the school, the students and, therefore, the context.

- People are on hand to offer ongoing support during the implementation phase.

- The input, and action resulting from the input, can be monitored and further inputs or adjustments made as necessary.

- A programme of training can be sustained over a period of time rather than being a one-off event.

External sources

Training from external sources does have a role to play, however.

- An external provider can offer a fresh perspective. It is easy for people to become 'institutionalized'. A different pair of eyes can sometimes help us see the wood from the trees.

- It is sometimes easier to ask the challenging question necessary for genuine improvement when you do not belong to an institution or work locally. The need to maintain good relationships is less of an issue for external providers.

- External providers often arrive free from baggage. When teachers already have an opinion about the worth of a trainer who they have encountered previously they can easily embark on a training session with a preconceived idea about the potential value of the training.

- External trainers can bring a wider view of developments that are taking place in other areas of the country.

- An external training input can still – indeed, should – be managed internally. The extent to which an external trainer can deliver context-specific training is highly dependent upon the internal diagnosis (phase one) and the training brief provided by the school.

Example of a support options matrix

Type of support	On-site	Off-site
Define standards of practice	<ul><li>writing a school teaching policy based on threshold, Ofsted/Estyn/PM standards</li><li>departmental reviews</li><li>common frameworks for lesson planning with observation sheets that mirror them</li><li>CPD portfolios</li><li>work scrutiny</li><li>standard operating procedures (SOPs)</li></ul>	<ul><li>LEA/national guidelines</li><li>Ofsted/ESTYN handbook</li><li>TTA standards</li></ul>
Exposure to good practice	<ul><li>peer observation</li><li>modelling</li><li>cross-faculty observation – a class you teach taught by someone else</li><li>exam/test moderation</li><li>moderation of work and marking</li><li>shadowing good practitioners</li><li>team teaching</li><li>joint planning, policy writing</li></ul>	<ul><li>leading teacher</li><li>beacon school</li><li>exam/test moderation</li></ul>
Preparatory training	<ul><li>induction handbook</li></ul>	<ul><li>LEA/cluster-based pre-HoD courses</li></ul>
Focuses in-service training	<ul><li>in-house cascade of INSET</li><li>use of school INSET days to address identified needs</li><li>teaching skills workshops</li><li>action research projects</li><li>student tracking</li><li>presenting to a staff/governors' meeting</li></ul>	<ul><li>external agency course</li><li>cross-school groups sharing ideas</li><li>action research projects</li><li>cluster-based INSET days</li><li>presenting to colleagues on an in-service session</li></ul>
Coaching/ mentoring	<ul><li>post-lesson wash-up and re-plan</li><li>post-observation support</li><li>role of SMT</li><li>role for ASTs</li><li>paired curriculum co-ordinators</li></ul>	<ul><li>teacher placements in business</li><li>training of trainers</li><li>LEA advisers</li></ul>
Develop networks	<ul><li>linking foundation to core subject faculty heads</li><li>cross-curricular focus groups</li><li>teaching and learning group</li></ul>	<ul><li>use of clusters to train, for example NQTs</li><li>cluster-based group of staff development tutors, subject leaders</li><li>specialist school/college networks</li><li>EAZ</li><li>internet</li><li>school improvement networks</li></ul>

Training for professional development

> **Perception is everything (page 29). What messages are sent by the way training is currently organized at your school?**
>
> **Is the emphasis on training for professional development or is there a perception that training involves being told to do something differently or better?**

We know that people will be more likely to change when they want to. People are also more likely to be receptive to change when they feel part of the process. There is a massive difference between the view that 'This is being done by *us* for *our* benefit' and '*They* are trying to make us change because they don't think we're good enough'. While these views represent the extreme positions, and most people's perception will lie somewhere along the continuum between the two, the general principle that training is more likely to be effective when it is viewed as a professional development, rather than as an accountability exercise holds true.

We are seeking to actively involve staff in the process and cultivate the perception that training is about professional development, and consequently for 'our benefit'. There are five main ways of involving staff in the process.

1 Planning training

Either ask a group of teachers to plan a training day or part of a training day, or issue all staff with a list of key issues that have cropped up during the year and ask them to tick which aspects of teaching and learning they would most like as the focus for a training day. (This provides them with a degree of choice and the *perception* of control – the bottom line is that there is going to be an INSET day on teaching and learning.)

2 Provide choice during the day

Run a training day that includes a series of workshops, with teachers opting to attend those that appeal to them the most. This is a subtle way of getting teachers to make a positive choice – 'I *want* to go to …'

Events such as these may involve a number of different providers. To make them cost-effective, organize them as a cluster or pyramid with other schools, which has the spin-off benefit of social and professional interaction between teachers from different organizations.

INSET days

A self-reflection exercise

How frequently do INSET days fulfil the following criteria?

1 = always,   2 = frequently,   3 = occasionally,   4 = never

(1) The focuses of INSET days are determined by systematic diagnoses. ☐

(2) INSET days focus upon specific aspects of teaching and learning. ☐

(3) Trainers are provided with a tight brief, intended training outcomes and relevant background information prior to planning the training session. ☐

(4) Teachers are involved in planning and delivering INSET days. ☐

(5) INSET days generate concrete strategies for the classroom. ☐

(6) Training has a strong subject-specific dimension. ☐

(7) Time is made available during or immediately after INSET days for teachers to write material and prepare resources. ☐

(8) INSET days are held at or near the beginning of term. ☐

(9) There is a requirement for teachers to act following an INSET day. ☐

(10) INSET days lead to changes in classroom practice. ☐

To what extent does your current training programme lead to *improvements* in the classroom? Award yourself a mark out of ten (ten being the top mark).

What is one thing you could do to raise your score by one mark?

3 Delivering training

Teachers can deliver training in their own school. This is different to simply providing feedback on a course that they have attended. There are a number of benefits to this approach.

- The training is likely to be highly context-specific.

- The process of planning and delivering training is likely to develop their understanding and expertise still further ('If you want to know a subject, teach it').

- If they are respected members of staff, they will have instant credibility – actually doing it in the classroom counts for much when working with teachers.

- They will already be implementing the training message with the children in their school. 'You can't do that with *our kids*' is a significant barrier to change. Teachers will be more likely to adopt an idea when they can see that it works – especially in the same school.

- They will be on hand to provide advice and support after the training day has finished.

Combining external with internal input combines the best features of context-specific internal training with external stimulus and support, and ensures that staff feel involved in the process. As such it is a potentially powerful model.

1   Schools diagnose the aspect of classroom practice they wish to tweak (phase one).

2   An external trainer provides intensive, high quality training for a team of between four and eight key teachers.

3   Each member of the team implements an agreed aspect of the training in his or her classroom.

4   This phase of trialling material can be combined with small-scale action research projects – are the tweaks impacting on learning?

5   A whole-staff training day is held, with the external trainer delivering a keynote address to set the context and generate some enthusiasm. This is followed by a series of workshops run by the team of teachers. It is context-specific training, focusing on strategies that have been developed and refined in situ. It is therefore part training and part dissemination of good practice.

4 During training

There are huge parallels between staff training and the way in which we teach children. Training, like learning, is an active process. Students need to grapple with and think about information in order to understand it. Above all, they must be engaged. So too must teachers be actively engaged during INSET.

Staff training is ultimately designed to help teachers develop their practice and enhance the quality of learning in the classroom. Teachers therefore need to understand and accept the need for development if they are to implement new ideas – at least with conviction – in the classroom.

Peer observation

- How many opportunities do younger staff have to observe more experienced colleagues in action?

- Do all staff have regular opportunities to observe teachers in different curriculum areas?

- Is it a requirement for teachers to observe colleagues in different subjects?

- Do all teachers have regular opportunities to observe colleagues with different learning or teaching styles?

- Have all your staff observed an excellent lesson?

- Do peer observations have a specific focus or agreed criteria?

How effective is your current peer observation programme? Award a mark out of ten (ten being the top mark).

What is one thing that you could do to raise your score by one mark?

5 Peer observation

Peer observation can be a highly effective source of training (Section Seven, *Case studies*, page 245). Teachers can learn much from each other, particularly when there is a specific focus to lesson observations and teachers are clear about what they are looking for. All schools have excellent teachers. More specifically, all schools have teachers who excel at various parts of the lesson or aspects of teaching. It can be highly productive to provide opportunities for a teacher seeking to tweak an aspect of his or her practice to observe a teacher who is particularly proficient at that particular aspect.

'Observation for development' is very different to 'observation for monitoring' and can require different documentation, procedures and schedules. As a rule of thumb, much can be gained when teachers have an opportunity to observe:

- an experienced or excellent teacher teaching their subject

- a group they teach being taught in another curriculum area

- someone who excels in the aspect of teaching in which they are relatively weak

- a teacher with a very different preferred learning or teaching style (page 69).

Teaching outside of subject specialism

A key part of the improvement process is to reflect on what we do and why we do it. After teachers have been teaching for a few years, however, much of what they do and say in the classroom is instinctive and habitual. While we all accept the value of critical reflection, few of us actually find the time to do it.

> As part of a structured programme to develop the quality of teaching in a school, each teacher was required to teach a couple of lessons outside of his or her subject specialism.
>
> 'That was the best maths lesson we've ever had' was the feedback received by a young history teacher after she had taught her first maths lesson.
>
> 'But I don't understand maths' exclaimed the history teacher in surprise.
>
> 'Nor do we' replied the students.
>
> You might almost add 'but the person who normally teaches us does, and she makes some assumptions about how much we understand'.

Release the creativity

- Work in cross-curricular groups of between four and six teachers.
- The first teacher outlines an area of his or her subject to be covered in a lesson, providing any necessary explanations, and briefing the group as to the intended learning outcomes.
- The group then plans the lesson. The specialist teacher is available to answer any subject-specific queries, but does not contribute to the planning. The idea is to come up with some creative and novel approaches for the classroom.

Imagine what a maths lesson planned by a musician, technology teacher, drama specialist and historian might look like!

The way that teachers choose to teach is the result of a number of variables: the time of the day, the weather, the age and ability of the students, and the particular focus of the lesson, to name but a few. However, at a much more fundamental level, there are a number of factors that have a significant influence on the way that a teacher behaves in the classroom. The fact that teachers are not always aware of the subtle influences at play is significant in itself.

These factors include:

- the way the teacher prefers to learn
- the way the teacher was taught
- the way the teacher was trained to teach
- the experiences the teacher had during their first teaching post.

However, one of the most significant influences on teachers in secondary schools is the fact that they are subject experts. Secondary teachers are looking through the eyes of a historian, musician or mathematician, for example, while the vast majority of the students they teach are not. It is easy – despite the best of intentions – for subject specialists to make some false assumptions about levels of basic understanding.

The following strategies can prove effective when trying to combat this effect.

- Arrange for all teachers to teach a few lessons in a significantly different curriculum area – it is one of the most effective reflective experiences that a teacher can have.

- Compare the data generated when these lessons are observed with the data generated when the teacher is teaching his or her specialism. An interesting area for discussion is the proportion of time spent in phase two of the lesson compared with phase three (page 140). Very often teachers spend significantly more time in phase three when teaching outside their specialism at the expense of lengthy periods of exposition. Why is this? Why do they spend longer in phase two when teaching their own subject – because they need to, or because they are able to?

- Attach teachers to different curriculum areas for planning purposes. Non-specialists adopt the role of the students. When the non-specialist says 'Hang on a moment, you've lost me at this point. I don't see how you get from A to B', there is every chance that some students would be experiencing a similar difficulty.

Timing

The timing of training is significant. Input, in whatever form, is not a one-off event. It is a stage in a process and, to have the desired effect, must be implemented in the classroom and become embedded in practice. Whether a training session, INSET day or peer observation takes place on a Monday or Friday and near the beginning or end of term will often affect the chances of teachers subsequently acting upon the stimulus.

The timing of training during the school year can also be significant. Many teachers spend the second half of the spring term collecting and marking coursework. Training sessions at this time of year – even when they are well received – are unlikely to make much of an impact in the classroom.

Swingometer

Change involves increasing the number of people influenced by a new idea – that is, moving the swingometer from position A (the status quo) to position E (all teachers implementing the new policy, strategy or approach).

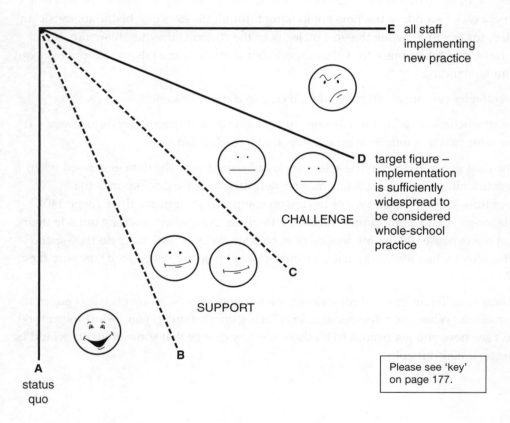

E all staff implementing new practice

D target figure – implementation is sufficiently widespread to be considered whole-school practice

CHALLENGE

C

SUPPORT

B

A status quo

Please see 'key' on page 177.

The line will move from A to B without the need for management action.

The line will move from B to C with support and persuasion.

The line will only move from C to D with challenge and support.

Phase three – implementation

We are now seeking to create the conditions that will make it more likely that teachers will implement the strategies devised in phase two in the classroom.

> The key to this phase is the management and support of senior members of staff. We are trying to persuade teachers to venture out of the comfort zone and to ensure that, having done so, they have a sufficiently positive experience to make them want to do it again.

This phase is unlikely to be effective when:

● it is not driven and managed by senior staff

● phase two (input) has failed to generate practical and specific strategies

● too much is attempted in one go

● there are other conflicting priorities.

This, in many respects, is the key phase. Although accurate diagnosis and high quality training significantly increase the chances of teachers developing their practice, these things by no means guarantee it. Few people leave the comfort zone of their own accord, thus – although practice varies considerably between schools – the implementation phase is often neglected. Indeed, an NFER research study conducted in 66 schools in the year 2000 found little evidence of follow-up activities between (INSET) days.

The challenge

The challenge is to get ideas introduced during training to be adopted by teachers and embedded in their daily practice. Consider the diagram opposite (borrowed from *Election Night Special*!).

Widespread change involves increasing the numbers of people adopting the new idea or approach (page 31), ideally from position A, which represents the status quo, to position E, representing the point at which *all* teachers are implementing the new policy or strategy.

However, for some schools, a more realistic aim would be for *most* teachers to be on board. Position D represents the point at which sufficient teachers have adopted the new practice for it to be considered as whole-school practice. Schools will have different views on what proportion of teachers – 90 per cent? 75 per cent? – represents a satisfactory 'critical mass', and should set the target figure (position D) accordingly. This figure will often depend on variables such as the size of the school and the precise nature of the strategy involved.

Positions B and C indicate that some staff have taken a new idea on board and implemented it in the classroom. However, the numbers are less than the agreed target figure – position D. It means that insufficient teachers are using the new strategy for it to make a widespread difference to practice.

Tapping the boulder

Three men were working in a quarry. The first was smashing a heavy sledgehammer repeatedly onto a large boulder. It was to no avail; the boulder stubbornly refused to crack. The man grew agitated but, determined not to be beaten, he continued to bring the sledgehammer crashing down onto the rock. Still the boulder did not crack.

The second man adopted a similar approach, wielding the heavy hammer high above his head before bringing it crashing down onto the boulder below. Less patient than his colleague, the second man hit the boulder only three or four times before accepting defeat and moving onto the next rock. New rock, same tactic, same result.

The third man was slumped against a wall, his exhausted and dispirited expression revealing that he too had hit many boulders. His discarded sledgehammer clearly indicated that he had concluded there was little point expending further energy on what had proved a futile task.

Meanwhile, a fourth man entered the quarry. He walked straight past the sledgehammer that was leaning against the wall awaiting his arrival, and instead picked up a small mallet. Slowly, he approached a boulder and examined it carefully. Finally, he tapped the boulder firmly just a couple of times. The boulder, unable to resist, let out a small sigh and began to crack. The noise grew louder as the split proceeded along its inevitable journey.

Moving the line

At the risk of oversimplifying the situation, teachers in most schools fall into four broad categories. Teachers will fall into different categories depending on the precise nature of the practice concerned. For example, a teacher who would warmly embrace any initiative to improve the quality of questioning in the classroom may be significantly less enthusiastic about incorporating ICT into his or her lessons.

Prior to a training event, most senior leadership teams could predict how individuals will respond, with a high degree of accuracy, and place members of their staff into the various categories accordingly.

Wildly enthusiastic

These are the enthusiasts who are open and receptive to any suggestion or new idea. They will invariably go away and try out new ideas in the classroom after a training session. Changes will take place with or without management action.

Generally receptive

These teachers are generally enthusiastic and receptive to new ideas but will not always get around to actually implementing new approaches. However, when they can see the merit of a proposal, they only require some encouragement, persuasion or cajoling to nudge them into action. Support is often sufficient for teachers in this category to change.

Significantly reluctant (key marginals)

These teachers are less than enthusiastic about changing. They are deeply rooted in their comfort zone and often display an attitude to change that ranges from reluctance to overt scepticism. These feelings stem from a variety of sources. However, they are often the manifestation of a fundamental lack of confidence and fear of change (page 41). Support alone will not persuade these teachers – the 'key marginals' – to change. Support *and* challenge are required to move teachers in this category.

Firmly entrenched (cynics!)

These teachers are deeply entrenched in their views. Scepticism has given way to full blown cynicism! For every silver lining, they can think of ten clouds! Even support and challenge – provided these teachers are operating at a satisfactory level – will often fail to bring about *significant* changes to teachers in this category.

Teachers in the middle ground – neither enthusiast nor cynic – are the key battleground. Win them over and a project gathers momentum and a new strategy becomes embedded. Fail to win them over …

The key marginals

● Success is often dependent upon winning over teachers – particularly influential members of staff – in the third category, the key marginals. In many respects, these teachers represent the crucial battleground. Gain their support and compliance and we establish sufficient support for a project to gather momentum and for a new strategy to become embedded. Fail to win them over, however, and any innovation is limited to isolated pockets and will invariably wither and peter out.

● Schools will have different proportions of teachers in each category. Some schools are blessed with large numbers of enthusiasts; other schools have more cynics. However, in most schools, there are insufficient teachers in the first two categories – enthusiastic and receptive – to represent a critical mass. Therefore, for an idea or new strategy to become adopted across the school (and for the agreed target figure to be achieved) a degree of challenge is required.

● Teachers who regularly teach excellent lessons are often the enthusiasts who embrace developments with an open mind and are keen to try out new ideas in the classroom. Similarly, there is often a strong correlation between teachers who fall into the key marginals category and those who are teaching satisfactory or good lessons. Without an element of challenge, therefore, excellent teachers get even better, while the teachers who we really need to develop remain largely unaffected by the process.

● In any staffroom there are members of staff whose opinion carries a great deal of weight, their acceptance or rejection of an idea often influencing a significant number of staff around them. When these people can be found in the third and fourth categories – key marginals and cynics – the challenge of widespread implementation is greatly enhanced. Identifying and moving these people (page 174) can go a long way to winning over a critical mass of teachers.

A managed process

Meeting the challenge of moving from good ideas at training events to implementation in the classroom is a managed process. The two basic ingredients are support – some teachers need considerable reassurance – and challenge – some teachers need anything from a nudge to a shove before they will leave their comfort zone and develop their practice.

While the ingredients may be apparent, there is, however, no single recipe that guarantees success during the implementation phase. Schools and the individuals in them are all different and so an approach that proves successful in one context will not necessarily work in another. Success in this phase is largely dependent upon skilful school leaders mixing and matching the available strategies to achieve the blend and balance of challenge and support required by different teachers and different circumstances.

What follows, then, is a list of suggestions and some general principles. They do not comprise an off-the-peg strategy solution or the 'correct approach'. They do, however, provide some food for thought and some concrete ideas that schools can adapt and adopt as appropriate.

Richmond School

Checklists of tasks for day 2

1   From the NOF Training Day, Thinking and Learning Day plus Literacy and Numeracy Strategy and Language for Learning Group, identify areas of development for Key Stage 3 within the department. This is to be included in the Department Development Plan.

2   Once the developments have been identified and agreed upon by the department, produce an action plan which outlines:

   ● the tasks that need to be done

   ● who is going to do each task

   ● the timescale by which each task will be completed

   ● the planned outcome for each task

   ● how the development will be monitored and evaluated (refer to Performance Management lesson observations and discussion within departments).

3   Identify two or three points in the year when the department will come together to:

   ● assess if the implementation of the work is on target and what (if any) modifications need to be made

   ● assess what has worked, what has not, and why

   ● assess whether remaining planned tasks need refining/changing in light of monitoring and evaluation to date

   ● assess whether the department needs additional input (from external or internal agencies) to take thinking further forward.

4   Complete the action plan, and the dates for follow-up work, and hand to PM by the end of the day. Link meetings in the spring and summer term will have Thinking and Learning as a standing agenda item. PM will make sure that link SMT receives the appropriate action plans.

5   Written feedback (A3 sheets) from each department will be displayed at the plenary session at the end of day 2. PM will collate the information and circulate to all staff. Whole-school issues will be addressed by the senior management and the extended management teams, and the outcomes will be reported back to all staff as soon as possible.

Thanks to Richmond School, North Yorkshire, for permission to reproduce this checklist.

Make it a requirement

> **After an INSET session, do you:**
> - hope that people will implement the ideas
> - expect them to do so
> - require them to do so?

When we set aside time during or immediately after a training event, and issue a checklist of *required* follow-up tasks such as the example opposite, it will significantly increase the chance of something happening as a result of the training.

Read through the example on page 180, opposite. Four features are worth noting.

1   Teachers are working in departments. Many people are reassured by working collaboratively. At a subconscious level, it is the department rather than the individual who is being asked to change.

2   The first line of challenge, support or influence is from a head of department. Teachers who are resistant to implementing 'commands from on high' may respond differently to a request from their head of department. The closer personal relationships that exist within a department *may* increase the chances of change – make the most of them.

3   Teachers and departments are provided with a choice. People – be they students or teachers – like to feel that they are in control and choosing to do something. Influence is subtle. Giving people a free choice, or a choice between X and Y, induces a positive 'I want to …' response, and the fact that they didn't want to change in the first place is often forgotten.

4   There is a clear expectation that developments are going to be made. There is a timescale and the whole process is overseen by an attached member of the senior team.

Commit to it

People are more likely to pursue and meet a target when they have committed to it – particularly when their intentions are made public. Design a pro-forma for departments or teachers to use to outline precisely what they intend to do. Make it detailed. Include a deadline. Copies of completed pro-formas should be collected by a line manager and posted on a staff notice board to keep everyone informed of developments that are taking place in the school. (An alternative adopted by at least one school is to put people in front of a video camera – almost as if they were joining a dating agency! Teachers simply say, 'By this date, I will have achieved or carried out this action.')

Have a deadline

If it doesn't have a deadline, it often doesn't get done. However *important* the matter, *urgent* issues – with a deadline – will always win the day (page 129). Short deadlines can be particularly effective.

'Start small; think big.'

David Perkins

Ask for regular updates

Use the regular line management meeting to ask for updates on progress. Make it a standing agenda item. Alternatively, send out a short pro-forma asking for a summary of what has been done, what has gone well, what is the next step, and so on, at appropriate intervals.

Implement immediately after training

People are more likely to introduce ideas from training immediately after the event. The following day or week is therefore crucial. If training is followed by a particularly busy period or a holiday, the chances of changes taking place are remote. The annual training programme must be planned in conjunction with the school calendar – avoid scheduling INSET in the week or two preceding parents' evenings or report writing, for example.

Chunk the challenge

Chunk the challenge, or – as David Perkins in *Smart Schools* puts it – 'Start small, think big'. If 'improving teaching and learning', or 'planning all lessons around multiple intelligences', is our ultimate goal, it is a daunting prospect. Reducing the size of the challenge takes a step-by-step approach to improvement, and as such is reassuring and realistic.

Chunking the challenge, involves:

- **developing a specific aspect at a time**. Breaking down a large, complex challenge into a series of manageable steps is the key to making progress. Often such small steps – introducing the phrase 'maybe … and' into teaching, for example – seem too small to make a difference, and almost inconsequential. However, any step in the right direction – however small – is progress.

  Possible aspects for development include questioning techniques, memory, motivation, thinking skills and plenary sessions, for example. The four-phase lesson model offers a structure to focus training. Concentrate on each phase in turn, generating, swapping and implementing specific strategies and tasks (page 137).

- **working with a specific year group or teaching group**. For many teachers, it is the prospect of losing control that is the source of their reluctance to change. Working with one group – particularly the group with which the teacher enjoys the best relationship – significantly reduces the fear factor.

When we combine these two dimensions, the prospect teachers face is of introducing just one strategy with one teaching group. This is a very different prospect to 'improving teaching'.

Making something the *sole* priority – even for a brief period – is not just about creating time for it. It is an emphatic statement:

This is important!

A common focus?

Schools need to decide whether to adopt a school, departmental or individual approach to the improvement process. This is a major decision, and there is no wrong or right answer. Each approach offers various advantages and much will depend upon the specific circumstances of the school.

A school approach involves all departments developing the same aspect at the same time – for example, 'The focus for this term is to develop the quality of tasks employed in phase three'. The advantages of this approach are:

● it generates a sense of whole-school improvement

● it is easier to plan training sessions, organize the school diary, and so on

● it increases the chances of sharing good ideas between curriculum areas

● there is a clear message that 'This is about improving *teaching*, not *teachers.*'

A departmental or individual approach involves departments or teachers focusing on different aspects of teaching. The key benefits of this approach are:

● departments or teachers will have *chosen* to focus upon a particular aspect

● departments or teachers can focus upon the specific aspect that they have identified as the bit *they* need to tweak.

A combination of these approaches could be adopted. For example, in term one the whole school could work upon a common focus for development, and then in term two each department could identify its own focus for development. Alternatively, the school could adopt a broad area for development, such as learning styles, for example. Departments and individuals could then choose a specific focus from within that broad area, such as multiple intelligences, or kinesthetic learners, for example.

Make it the sole priority

Whichever approach is adopted, the chances that an issue will be successfully addressed and new approaches introduced into the classroom will be significantly increased if that issue is made the *sole* priority. It is a principle that applies equally to schools, departments and individuals. The length of time is less important than making a timeslot sacrosanct: the new strategy or approach could be the focus for the academic year or sole priority for the term. Equally, it could be the priority of the week, the day or the sole agenda item of a meeting.

A key barrier to change is conflicting priorities. Although we have little choice but to respond to a range of initiatives – many of which are externally imposed – during the course of an academic year, it is possible to address them one at a time. More progress can sometimes be made in a week when we adopt a sole focus approach than during a term when conflicting demands constantly erode time and energy.

Depersonalize the issue. Focus on strategies, not people – on teaching, not teachers. 'That strategy that *we* developed last week wasn't as effective as *we* thought it would be', is a very different message to '*You* taught a lousy lesson'.

Making an issue a *sole* priority means that, for the designated period:

- it is the focus for all meetings
- all INSET days and training sessions are devoted to it
- it is an agenda item on all line management meetings
- report writing, mock examinations, marking of coursework, and so on, are not scheduled for this period
- it is the focus for all lesson observations and feedback sessions.

Work collaboratively

As a general principle, teams of teachers are more likely to introduce new ideas than individuals. Teams provide a mutual support network that is especially valuable when developments hit a snag or resolve is tested. There is something particularly reassuring about knowing that 'I am not in this alone'. There is also a subtle message that a programme is about improving teaching – however good it already is – rather than about improving just '*my* teaching'.

The key benefits of working collaboratively include the following.

- More ideas are generated by a group than by an individual.
- Problems encountered and issues arising in the classroom can be addressed together.
- There is an emotional support network – everyone is facing a similar challenge.
- Momentum can be generated and maintained – a teacher who is flagging can be re-energized at a team meeting by colleagues (enthusiasm is infectious).
- There are opportunities for team teaching.
- The focus is on strategies, not people.
- A team is likely to include teachers with different learning styles and teaching approaches.

Focusing upon strategies is often crucial to the success of developing classroom practice. There are at least four reasons for this.

1 Although strategies are principally generated during input and training, the process of identifying and sharing good ideas for lessons will continue during the implementation phase. As a basic rule, the more strategies that can be identified, the more chance there is of a teacher finding one with which he or she is comfortable.

2 As strategies are implemented in the classroom for the first time, they will almost certainly be evaluated and refined accordingly.

3 Teachers will be more likely to implement a strategy when they are convinced that it will work. When members of a department announce that they tried an activity and it went really well, the chances of other teachers giving it a go are greatly enhanced.

4 Placing the emphasis on strategies depersonalizes the entire process and places the focus upon *teaching* rather than *teachers*. 'That strategy that *we* developed last week wasn't as effective as *we* thought it would be', carries a very different message and a very different level of threat to '*You* taught a lousy lesson.'

None of us is as smart as all of us.

Japanese proverb

Team teaching

Team teaching not only provides the support of an extra adult (page 193), it dilutes the threat. It is 'we' who are 'on trial', not 'I'. There are a number of variations on the team teaching theme. They all offer a degree of reassurance as we seek to both support teachers and keep the focus on strategies and not people. For example:

- 'I plan – you teach.'

- 'You plan – I teach.'

- 'We plan – we teach (either separate classes or as a team teaching exercise).'

Team planning

Plan a single lesson as a department. All members of the department then teach the lesson to different groups. Hold a debriefing meeting to evaluate the strategies. For example, what worked well? What were the less successful aspects?

Alternatively, plan a *series* of lessons as a department using some new ideas or techniques. Each member of the department then contracts to teach one of the lessons. Hold a debriefing meeting as above.

Use a coach

Attach an internal coach, external adviser or advanced skills teacher to a department, to assist in the team planning scenarios outlined above. Not only do you benefit from their experience and expertise, but people are more likely to do something if they know that a coach or adviser is returning on a certain date for the debriefing session.

Demonstrate good practice

Convincing teachers that new ideas and approaches are not only effective learning strategies but also workable in the classroom is a major challenge for those school leaders attempting to develop practice. Teachers are therefore much more likely to try something new when they have seen it working in the classroom.

Coaches can be used to teach demonstration lessons and teachers can be given opportunities to see colleagues in action. Make these observations specific. Teachers need to observe the particular strategy that they are considering adopting. There are two key benefits to this approach.

1   Teachers should be crystal clear about exactly how to implement a new strategy.

2   Teachers will have seen it working with 'our kids'.

Many teachers have never had the opportunity to observe an excellent lesson – yet we all expect them to be able to teach one.

Attach a line manager to a department

Attaching a coach to a department for collaborative planning or teaching is a highly supportive strategy. When a situation requires a higher degree of challenge, however, attach a line manager to the department instead of, or in addition to, a coach. It provides a different emphasis.

While the precise role of the line manager may vary with context, the overall brief is to keep the project at the top of the agenda and generally drive the implementation process. He or she can attend planning sessions during and after training events, observe the new strategies being tried in the classroom and regularly review progress with the head of department during line management meetings. It is a very effective strategy when the particular situation calls for a high degree of management.

Attach a teacher with a different teaching approach to a department

Accommodating different types of learner in the classroom is difficult, not least because it is very hard to imagine precisely how someone with a very different learning style than your own prefers to work. Many logical, step-by-step learners, for example, would be amazed just how restrictive a random processor finds this way of working. Similarly, many intuitive, tangential thinkers would struggle to provide the structure needed by linear, sequential thinkers, simply because that is not how they think.

When all members of a department share a similar learning style – and probably, therefore, a similar teaching approach – they would benefit from the input and support of a teacher with a significantly different learning preference. The grid on page 70 can be used as a whole-school resource. Use it to identify a teacher who works in a very different manner to teachers in a particular curriculum area and attach that person to the team for planning and training purposes.

Develop the students

If you are trying to introduce a new skill or approach into the classroom, it can sometimes be worthwhile to develop the particular skill with a group of students first. For example, if you are keen to develop the use of learning maps in the classroom, but find that teachers are reluctant to use them, teach the skill to a group of students independently. There are two main benefits.

1   Students may well ask if they can portray a particular piece of information in map form. Students thus become the catalyst for change.

2   The challenge has been halved – or at least reduced. Teachers are not required to teach the process and incorporate the technique into their lessons. Students already have the skill – all the teacher has to do is make use of it.

People are more likely to change when they want to and feel that change is for their benefit.

Therefore, provide as much choice – or perceived choice – as possible before, during and after training.

Choice is empowering. When presented with a choice, people are required to make a positive decision. It is a subtle but powerful message – 'I am doing this because I want to'.

Swap groups

Swapping groups is an extension of the idea of developing the students. As part of a *planned* strategy, teacher A introduces an approach with a particular class, possibly during the summer term – for example, students using learning logs to reflect upon their learning and review work at the end of lessons. Gradually the students become used to the approach until it becomes second nature to them.

Deliberately timetable this class with a different teacher for the new academic year (one who is a little unsure of adopting the approach in their own lessons). When the teacher asks the group to fill in their learning logs at the end of the first lesson, the students will know exactly what to do.

Provide support for the team

Teachers frequently complain that, in recent years, they have been asked to implement new courses, syllabuses and approaches without being given the necessary time and resources to do the job. Not only is it a legitimate complaint, it is how they feel and therefore is a potential barrier to development.

Providing each department with a supply day to be taken soon after each INSET day, to assist in the implementation of the new ideas in the classroom, does several things.

1   It sends some clear messages:

   ● This is important.

   ● It is so important that it is being backed with resources.

   ● You are professionals and we are treating you as such.

2   It gives the department a degree of control and ownership of the process. They are choosing how to spend the supply cover.

3   It negates the 'we haven't got time' defence.

Provide support for the individual

When a teacher leaves the comfort zone and tries out a new idea for the first time, they are working in what Christopher Bowring-Carr and John West-Burnham call the 'zone of uncertainty'. Not only are they likely to be a little tentative and uncertain, they will be operating at a conscious level (page 21).

The prospect of having another adult in the classroom while they introduce a new technique often tips the balance between thinking about doing something and actually giving it a go. It also increases the chances that the first experience of a new strategy will be positive. It is counter-productive to persuade someone to leave their comfort zone only for them to have a disastrous experience – if that happens, the chances of their trying the technique again are just about nil! Getting teachers out of the comfort zone is only the first step; the real challenge is getting them to redefine it (page 19).

The zone of uncertainty

the zone of uncertainty
the comfort zone

When teachers leave the comfort zone, they enter the zone of uncertainty. (As they do so, they bear a striking resemblance to Bambi on ice!)

Not only are they likely to be a little tentative, they will also be operating at a conscious level (page 21).

As they become increasingly familiar and comfortable with a new strategy, they will gradually redefine their comfort zone and the new practice will become part of the norm.

Note

There are huge parallels between the zone of uncertainty and the zone of proximal development (page 52).

The supporting teacher has four main effects.

1   Teachers are more likely to go through with something having arranged for another teacher to come in. No last minute changes of mind!

2   The presence of an extra adult reduces the risk of poor behaviour. Equally significantly, the teacher concerned *thinks* it does.

3   The additional adult presence allows teachers to concentrate a little more on the new strategy – that is, work at a conscious level – rather than on the class.

4   The extra teacher acts as observer and can provide useful feedback after the event.

A few further points are worth.

● Not all teachers welcome the presence of another adult as they try something for the first time. Many would take the view that 'If I'm going to make a fool of myself, I would rather not have another adult there to witness the event!'

● Who would you rather have in the classroom with you as you risk 'coming a cropper' – your line manager or your friend? On many occasions it is a senior member of staff who is available to act as support. However, for some teachers, this is the last person they would choose.

● The key is that teachers have a choice. Support must be available *if they want it*. They must also be able, at least on occasions, to nominate who they would like to support them. It can be the difference between their trying something out or not.

● We have all heard people say 'Just shout if you need a favour'. We have never taken them up on their offer because we don't want to be a nuisance or because something about the way they said it gives us the impression that they don't really mean it. There is a massive difference between a deputy head saying at a staff meeting 'Please let me know if you would like some support in the classroom when you try this out', and approaching a teacher in the corridor, looking genuinely interested and saying 'I notice that you have Year 8 tomorrow period 3 – I'm free then and it would be a perfect opportunity to try out that strategy that **we** were discussing yesterday. It's OK if I come in and support then, isn't it?'

Make it school policy

Making an approach school policy does not guarantee that all teachers will adopt it, but it does make it more likely. In particular, it significantly increases the chances that the teachers who require more than just support to do something will give it a go.

Provided that teachers have been part of the process, and the issue has been properly discussed, making something school policy can be enough to persuade teachers in the 'key marginals' category (page 177) to implement a new approach, thus moving the swingometer past the target position and establishing something as school-wide practice (page 174). There are some teachers who, even when they dislike or disagree with an approach, will comply and implement it the minute it becomes school policy.

Reviewing the impact of tweaking 'closes the loop' and leads directly back into the diagnosis phase.
Thus improving the quality of teaching becomes a continuous cycle.

Phase four – review

Having tweaked, we must now close the loop and ask two questions.

1   Is everybody doing it?

2   Is it improving learning?

This phase is unlikely to be effective when:

- it is neglected!

- senior staff *assume* that tweaks have been made and that teachers have made changes to their classroom practice

- phases one, two and three have been unsuccessful.

In the same way that teachers cannot assume that students have understood information just because their exposition has been of high quality, school leaders cannot assume that teachers have taken on board new ideas and developed their practice, just because they have provided high quality training.

Reviewing the impact of training is an essential, but easily neglected, final phase of the improvement loop. It involves the dimensions of both monitoring ('Are we doing what we said we would?') and evaluation ('Is it *improving* learning?'), and is equally applicable for individuals, curriculum areas or the whole school.

The key issues

- What evidence or data are we going to use in the review phase? To what extent do we involve students in the review process? Have they noticed a difference in the way they are taught? Has it helped them learn?

- What do we now see in lessons that we didn't see prior to tweaking?

- Are teachers consistently implementing the agreed tweaks? How do we know?

- How much progress have we made with the swingometer (page 174)? That is, to what extent have changes in classroom practice become embedded? What proportion of the staff are implementing the strategy on a regular and frequent basis?

- How does this compare with the target set before the training phase commenced?

- How effective have the tweaks been at improving learning and raising achievement? How do we know?

- What refinements (tweaks to the tweaks) do we need to make?

- How quickly do we review? It is unlikely that new ideas will be effective immediately. Change takes time. It may be necessary for an interim review (for example, 'Early signs are encouraging but it is too early to assess the impact of the changes on achievement'), with a follow-up review when attainment data becomes available.

- Review is part of an ongoing process and leads back into the diagnosis phase. Thus improving teaching and learning becomes a continuous cycle.

Of all the changes that are taking place in education, the shift in emphasis from INSET to coaching is potentially the most exciting and significant.

Section Five

Coaching

This Section covers the following key points.

■ What is coaching?

■ The coaching loop (DIIR)

Professional development, although often organized collectively, is largely a personal process, the precise aspect of teaching that would benefit from tweaking often varying considerably between teachers, even those in the same department. We have long recognized the value of differentiating the learning experience for students, yet, rather ironically, staff training days rarely account for variations in staff experience, expertise and need.

Understandably, therefore, there is growing interest in the notion of individual coaching or mentoring and the role that such a process can play in improving teaching. Indeed, of all the changes that are currently taking place in the world of education, the shift in emphasis from INSET to coaching is potentially one of the most exciting and significant.

What is coaching?

Coaching involves a professional guide or mentor working intensively with an individual or small group of teachers to help them develop their practice. The key role of the coach, therefore, is to help people move out of the comfort zone without feeling (too) uncomfortable.

Key features

● Coaching is more than training, as it establishes a personal tweaking–feedback–tweaking loop that involves all four phases – diagnosis, input, implementation, review – of the DIIR improvement process (page 149). As such, it can provide highly specific input or training geared to the strengths, weaknesses and stage of development of the individual.

● Coaching is ongoing. The DIIR model is a loop. Each feedback and review session offers the potential for further tweaking.

● Coaching is equally applicable to teachers who are teaching satisfactory lessons and those who are teaching excellent ones.

● Coaching is more than professional guidance. Good coaching also provides the support and reassurance that many teachers need before they will try out new ideas in the classroom.

The best coaches in sport are motivators – they instil confidence, belief and enthusiasm. Why should it be any different in education?

- Coaching is a long-term investment, not a quick fix solution. The foundations of successful coaching are personal relationships. Mutual respect and, above all, trust are the key ingredients of successful coaching and genuine professional growth.

- Coaching is non-judgemental. The emphasis is very much on professional development rather than accountability.

Professional and personal

Coaching operates at two levels:

1   professional guidance – advice on teaching techniques and strategies

2   emotional support and reassurance.

As such, it has the potential to address two of the key barriers to developments in classroom practice:

- a failure to translate *generic* training into appropriate strategies for *specific* situations

- a lack of confidence to implement new techniques in the classroom.

Professional guidance

All teachers benefit from professional advice and ongoing, high quality training. The more strategies that teachers have at their disposal, the better. When teachers fail to translate generic training into concrete strategies that will work in their classroom, the chances of training having a significant impact on classroom practice are slight.

INSET, simply because it is delivered to large numbers of teachers, is often too general to be highly effective. Teachers are concerned about specifics – a particular group, an individual student or a particular aspect of content, for example. Coaching can be more effective than traditional INSET, simply because it is highly context-specific and addresses individual professional needs.

Emotional support

However, the root cause of an individual's reluctance to change is often a lack of confidence. It is both significant and ironic that the same limiting beliefs and 'I can't do …' attitudes that so often hold students back and limit their learning frequently hold teachers back and limit their professional development.

If teachers believe that they couldn't implement a particular strategy, or that 'It wouldn't work with our kids', then it is extremely unlikely that they will give it a go. Even when they are prepared to try something, it is unlikely to be effective unless it is done with conviction.

A key role of a coach is to help people address the factor that is preventing them from developing. If it is a lack of specific strategies, they must provide some; if it is a lack of confidence, they must provide the emotional support necessary for teachers to try something different. The best coaches in sport are motivators; they instil confidence, belief and enthusiasm. Why should it be any different in education?

It is not coaching that will bring about improvements in classroom practice. It is high quality coaching.

Good coaching

Just as the best players don't always make the best managers, the best teachers don't necessarily make the best coaches. Good coaching is dependent upon four factors:

1   **professional knowledge** – what learning is, what makes an excellent lesson, knowledge of a wide range of effective teaching strategies

2   **professional skills** – observation skills, feedback techniques

3   **professional judgement** – knowing when to push, when to back off, and so on

4   **personal qualities** – a good listener, optimistic, reassuring, has ability to influence, honesty, integrity.

Coaching the coaches

There is a training implication here: even coaches who are highly experienced teachers with extensive knowledge and finely honed professional skills can be improved. Coaching requires a significant investment in terms of time and money – investment that is wasted unless the process brings about improvement. It therefore makes sense to invest further in the professional development of the coaches. It is not coaching that will bring about improvements in classroom practice; it is *high quality coaching*.

A training checklist for coaches would probably include the following.

- Learning: a familiarity with the latest developments in the field of learning
- Teaching: a clear understanding of what constitutes excellent teaching, and the difference between a good lesson and an excellent one

    awareness of an extensive range of classroom strategies

    ability to demonstrate and model good practice
- Observation: precise identification of the bit to tweak
- Feedback: although offering advice in a non-threatening manner is partly dependent upon personality, there are techniques and approaches that can be taught to increase the effectiveness of feedback
- Motivation: good coaches *motivate* – effective motivation is partly dependent on personal characteristics and partly on learned techniques
- Influence: essentially coaching is about *influence* – it is easy to outline a strategy to teachers; it is a different challenge altogether to get them to believe that they could use it.

Coaches provide both professional guidance and personal support. They are there to bounce ideas off, make suggestions and provide encouragement and reassurance. Remember – coaches need coaches too!

The coaching loop

The coaching loop mirrors the improvement loop outlined on page 148 and involves four broad stages – diagnoses, input, implement, review (DIIR). However, coaching is the deluxe model; confidence, reassurance and support come as standard.

Many of the principles that underpin the various phases of the DIIR model apply to coaching; for example, observation must be specific in order to precisely diagnose the bit to tweak. However, as coaching operates at an individual level, there are some subtle but significant differences. This Section concentrates on those differences – the factors that distinguish coaching from INSET. It is offered as no more than a brief summary.

Coaching is an ongoing process in which the coach helps the 'coachee' to develop his or her practice. It is distinguished from more traditional forms of INSET by:

● personal relationships

● professional dialogue

● modelling

● professional and personal support.

Personal relationships

Section Three highlighted the significance of the emotional state of the students in the learning process. To paraphrase the Eric Jensen quote on page 57, unless the learner is in an appropriate state to learn, forget it – you're wasting your time. So too with coaching; if the teacher is not in an appropriate state to receive feedback, it is similarly a waste of time. The way in which teachers approach coaching – their emotional state – will be influenced by a great many factors – personal circumstances, the subtle messages that surround the whole coaching initiative and, not least, the relationship he or she enjoys with the coach.

A healthy relationship based upon mutual trust and respect is therefore not an optional extra for coaching; it is a prerequisite. The onus is, therefore, on the coach to consciously build the relationship, rather than leave it to chance. At a practical level, it involves taking an interest in the teacher's family, hobbies and interests as well as their professional development.

Provided that this interest is genuine, sincere and expressed with congruence, it will go a long way to creating a suitable atmosphere for professional development.

Every subtle message given out by the coach and the way the programme is managed at school level must reinforce the principle that the core reason for coaching programmes is individual professional development. If teachers – for whatever reason – believe or even suspect that the process, despite the rhetoric, is really about accountability and that private conversations and experiences in the classroom will be reported back to line managers, it is highly unlikely that they will be prepared to take the risks necessary for real professional growth.

A useful exercise is to present teachers with a set of data relating to a lesson that they have taught (for example, length of time in introduction, balance of open/closed questions, balance of questions addressed to boys/girls) and ask them how they would feed back to a teacher who had generated those statistics.

It is an attempt to depersonalize the issue and focus on the teaching, not the teacher.

Professional dialogue

People are more likely to change when they want to, or at least accept the need to develop. Therefore, the emphasis in coaching is on professional dialogue, rather than one-way feedback. Professional dialogue differs from feedback in that it is not judgemental. It is a professional conversation in which the coach is trying to help the teacher understand how his or her approach to teaching impacts on students' learning and what he or she could do in order to be more effective in the classroom.

It is highly skilled and involves providing information and asking questions that encourage teachers to reflect upon and talk about their practice. Coaches essentially do three things:

1   hold up a mirror so that teachers can see clearly what they do in the classroom

2   help teachers identify aspects of their practice that they wish to develop – he bit to tweak

3   help teachers to identify the way forward.

Holding up a mirror

What teachers think they do and what they actually do in the classroom are often two entirely separate things. 'Holding up a mirror' involves giving factual, rather than judgemental, feedback – for example, 'Your introduction lasted 22 minutes, you asked 18 questions, 2 of which were directed towards a girl and 16 directed at a boy'.

Often information of this kind is sufficient for teachers to recognize an area for development. Teachers don't need to be told that a gender split of 2:16 is less than ideal – they just need to be presented with the data.

Identifying the bit to tweak

Essentially, this is the diagnosis phase. However, the emphasis in coaching is on the teacher identifying the aspect of his or her own practice that would benefit from a tweak, rather than being told. The role of the coach is to guide the teacher through this process by asking a series of questions that enable the teacher to reflect upon his or her practice and probe the thinking behind it. Prompts used might include, for example:

● 'What made you decide to …?'

● 'Can you explain the thinking behind …?'

● 'Did it go as well as you had hoped?'

● 'If you were teaching the same lesson again, would you use the same approach?'

● 'How would you do it differently?'

● 'What would have been the effect of …?'

● 'What did you expect to happen when …?'

● 'How else could you have approached it?'

Useful strategies for the modelling phase

- coach plans – coach teaches

- joint planning – coach teaches

- teacher plans – coach teaches

- joint planning – teacher teaches part of the lesson

- joint planning – teacher teaches entire lesson

- teacher plans and teaches entire lesson.

Identifying the way forward

Coaches do not simply tell teachers how to teach. Coaching involves two professionals bouncing ideas off each other in order to agree on a way forward. In a sense, the coach becomes a personal sounding board for the teacher to help clarify his or her thinking. Liberal use of the word 'we' emphasizes the collaborative and developmental nature of the process. For example, 'How could *we* approach this?' or '*We* could give this a go – what do you think?' carry a very different message from '*You* need to improve'.

There will of course be occasions when a coach needs to provide some fresh ideas and offer a suggested approach for the classroom. There is an important balance to be established. Teachers do not want to simply be *told* how to teach – we must avoid an 'I know more than you' message at all costs. However, teachers need to have confidence in their coach and feel that he or she has something extra to offer them.

Two strategies are useful here.

1   Depersonalize the suggestion – avoid 'I do this and know all the answers' messages. Instead, use phrases like 'Some people tell me this is helpful in these situations – what do you think?' or 'I've seen that work well before – I've never tried it myself. Shall we give it a go?'

2   Provide an element of choice – for example, 'Strategy A might be suitable for situations like this or we could try strategy B – which one do you think will work best with that group?' Giving teachers alternatives in this way gives them the feeling of control and requires them to make a positive choice.

Modelling

Good coaches often model the new practice for the teacher. You would expect a tennis coach to be able to demonstrate a topspin backhand – why should it be different in the classroom? Modelling is a powerful and often under-used training technique. It is both reassuring and helpful for teachers to see precisely what a particular strategy 'looks like' in the classroom and that it actually works with 'our kids'!

There are two potential spin-off benefits from modelling.

1   It can add to the credibility of the coach. It is not a bad message that the person offering you support and professional guidance can actually hack it in the classroom!

2   Modelling gives the teacher a chance to provide feedback to the coach. It is a clear message that this is a professional partnership and that receiving feedback is part of a developmental process. If the coach is open to receiving feedback without being defensive, it is more likely that the teacher will be.

Coaching	INSET
● relevant to individual	● relevant to group
● subject-specific	● generic
● precise	● often general
● individual diagnoses	● no or collective diagnoses
● context-specific strategies	● often generic strategies
● guarantees support during implementation	● possible support during implementation
● individual feedback	● no feedback
● ongoing	● one-off
● professional advice and personal support	● professional advice

Personal and professional support

For many teachers the presence of an additional adult in the classroom when they leave the comfort zone is hugely reassuring (page 193). Indeed, tangible support is sometimes what makes the difference between a teacher trying a strategy and just talking about it. The difference with coaching is that the teacher has probably already supported the coach during the modelling phase. The fact that the coach has already been prepared to expose his or her teaching to public scrutiny further adds to the feeling of security and mutual support.

Professional development, however, involves individuals voluntarily leaving the comfort of their familiar practice and laying their professional credibility on the line. It is a process that many teachers feel may find them wanting. Personal and professional support is, therefore, much more than lending a hand in the classroom.

The role of the coach mirrors that of the teacher. Teachers need to create the conditions in which children are more likely to feel good about themselves and believe that they can succeed. So too must the coach.

Good coaches smile, reassure, use positive language, pick people up when they are down and leave them feeling energized and enthused. They know when to push and when to back off, when to praise and when to challenge, when to talk and when to listen. Above all, good coaches leave teachers with self-esteem not just intact, but positively enhanced.

Coaching takes time

Coaching cannot be rushed. It does not offer quick fix solutions, not least because it is heavily dependent upon the personal relationship of coach and teacher. Although occasionally two people hit it off immediately, it often takes time to develop the trust and respect necessary for significant change.

Coaching is an ongoing process and, as such, offers the opportunity for teachers to redefine rather than just venture out of their comfort zone. One of the main barriers to change and developments in classroom practice is that habits are so hard to break. A teacher may try out a new idea after training but will often quickly slip back into familiar practice. When a coach works with an individual over a period of time, he or she has an opportunity to help the teacher embed a particular way of working into the daily classroom routine.

Coaching can be expensive. Understandably there is a temptation to ask a coach to work with a teacher for a couple of weeks before turning their attention elsewhere. Occasionally a couple of weeks is enough – teachers may simply need to observe a technique in the classroom, or to have some professional reflection time, before they feel comfortable about moving on. Frequently, however, coaches need an extended period of time – weeks, months, even terms – to make a difference.

Self-reflection exercise for heads of department

1 = strongly agree,   2 = broadly agree
3 = broadly disagree   4 = strongly disagree

(1) I consistently challenge mediocrity. ☐

(2) Learning issues account for the majority of departmental meeting time. ☐

(3) I am clear in my own mind about the difference between a satisfactory lesson and an excellent one. ☐

(4) All members of my department are clear about the difference between a satisfactory lesson and an excellent one. ☐

(5) Practice changes after I have observed a lesson and given feedback. ☐

(6) I am comfortable giving feedback to members of my department. ☐

(7) I am comfortable giving negative feedback to members of my department. ☐

(8) Teachers in my department would say that learning is my number one priority. ☐

(9) I feel confident giving teachers advice about how to improve their teaching. ☐

(10) I am clear about the relative strengths and weaknesses of members of my department. These views are based upon evidence. ☐

(11) I have established a mechanism for sharing good ideas

(a) within this department ☐

(b) with other departments. ☐

Section Six

The role of middle managers

This Section covers the following key points.

■ The role of middle managers – 'heads of department' to 'subject leaders'

■ Training for middle managers

What role do your middle managers (heads of department, or subject leaders) currently play in *improving* the quality of teaching in their curriculum area?

How effective are they at improving the quality of teaching in their curriculum area?

In recent years there has been, in many schools, a significant shift in emphasis in the role of middle mangers, as heads of department have gradually evolved into subject leaders. It is more than a change of title; it is a subtle but significant change in emphasis that recognizes the key role that middle mangers can play in improving the quality of teaching and learning.

It is not, however, a role that all heads of department are comfortable with. Some are unwilling to intervene in the classroom practice of their close colleagues, many of whom are also personal friends. Others are, or at least feel, ill-equipped for the role and unable to carry it out effectively.

Their reluctance is understandable. Where once they ordered the stationery and organized the stock, they are now being asked to observe their colleagues and provide them with feedback on their performance. It is a significant change. As middle managers are given greater responsibility for improving the quality of teaching in their department, they are increasingly involved in helping their colleagues change and move out of the comfort zone – which of course requires them to change and leave theirs.

And 'change' is the key word. Change is difficult; change, for many, is threatening. It involves conscious effort and a balance of challenge and support. Many people will have read Section Two, *What do we know about change?*, in the context of improving the quality of teaching. It could equally apply to changing the role and raising the quality of middle management.

We cannot just expect middle managers to be able to play a leading role in improving teaching standards any more than we can demand that teachers teach excellent lessons. If we want teachers to improve we must provide training and support and gradually develop the quality of teaching as part of a managed process. The same is true for the quality of middle management.

It is an investment well worth making. Heads of department or team leaders are closer to their team members than senior school leaders and therefore often in a better position to influence

- To what extent are your middle managers engaged in monitoring the quality of teaching in their curriculum areas?

- To what extent are they engaged with coaching teachers in their departments?

- Are they aware of the difference?

- If heads of department are deployed primarily in a monitoring role, who does the coaching?

- If heads of department are deployed primarily as coaches, who monitors?

- What is the relationship between the head of department, the teacher, the coach and the line manager?

- Would all members of staff respond to these questions in the same way?

them. This includes the potential to influence the way in which they operate in the classroom. Not surprisingly, therefore, recognizing and exploiting the potential of middle managers is a key strand in a school's overall strategy for improving the quality of teaching and learning.

In order to maximize the impact of middle managers, two important factors must be borne in mind:

1   clarifying the role

2   providing high quality training.

Clarifying the role

> **How would your heads of department respond to the question 'What is your key role in this school?'**
>
> **Would they all give the same answer?**
>
> **Would it include reference to the quality of teaching and standards of achievement in their curriculum area?**

Monitoring or coaching?

One of the key decisions for a school when clarifying the role of middle managers is to determine the relationship between monitoring and coaching. To what extent are heads of department being asked to monitor the quality of teaching in their curriculum area, and to what extent are they being asked to coach teachers in their department?

There is no right answer. Both monitoring and coaching are essentially about promoting high quality teaching; both are necessary ingredients in the drive to improve classroom practice. However, the emphasis and approach of the two are very different and it is *crucial* that heads of department know exactly what is being asked of them. It is equally important that teachers in the department are clear about the role. When they are observed by their head of department, is it for accountability purposes or is it for their professional development?

There are significant overlaps, of course, between monitoring and coaching and heads of department can clearly perform both functions. Worthwhile monitoring must surely include an improvement dimension and a sense of progress, and this in turn requires that there is an element of coaching in any observation and feedback programme.

It is, however, precisely because the boundaries between monitoring and coaching are so blurred that the role of the head of department needs to be clarified. Individual schools need to consider the issue carefully. Consider the questions on the opposite page. Different schools in different circumstances and with different priorities will inevitably answer them differently. The answers do not matter; what matters is the fact that everyone in the institution knows them.

The role of middle managers is changing significantly as heads of department evolve into subject leaders. As they assume greater responsibility for teaching quality in their department, they are increasingly involved in helping teachers leave their comfort zone. This, of course, requires them to leave theirs.

Roles and responsibilities

The following is a checklist of some of the key roles and responsibilities of middle managers in relation to improving teaching and learning in their departments.

Effective middle managers/subject leaders:

- set the standard
- set the target
- keep the focus on teaching and learning
- ensure that good ideas are shared
- provide opportunities for teachers to observe good practice
- identify the bit to tweak
- provide feedback.

Setting the standard

Heads of department set the tone and set the standard. They do not need to be the best teachers but must be aware that if they do it in their classroom, they send a clear message to the rest of the department that it is acceptable practice.

Setting the target

Teachers will probably have discussed at school level what an excellent lesson 'looks like'. There is, however, a subject-specific dimension to the notion of excellent practice. It is the responsibility of the head of department to ensure that all teachers know precisely what constitutes excellence in their particular curriculum area.

Keeping the focus on teaching and learning

If the head of department does not keep the focus on teaching and learning, who does? The relative importance of teaching and learning will be reflected in the way in which a department spends meeting time. Although this will be influenced by whole-school policy, the head of department plays a significant role. The following are useful strategies to keep learning high on the agenda.

- Include a learning or 'good ideas' slot on every departmental meeting agenda.
- Include an 'I tried _____ this week' slot on every agenda.
- Include a 'lesson of the week' slot on every agenda. Select a lesson at random by choosing a day, period and teacher. Spend ten minutes collectively generating ideas for how the content due to be covered could be delivered.
- Deal with administration at the end of the meeting. (Admin matters will take ten minutes when they begin at 4.50pm but will take 45 minutes when they begin at 3.30pm!)
- Adopt a pro-forma for meetings that includes the prompt 'This meeting will improve the quality of learning in the classroom because: …' If the team cannot complete the sentence, the meeting does not go ahead.

Pair subject leaders to act as mutual critical friends. It is a particularly effective strategy when people are paired with a colleague who has different strengths and a different leadership style.

- Issue a weekly admin newsletter to reduce the amount of time taken up by admin matters in departmental meetings. (Keep a document on the departmental computer that all members of the team can add to. Print and distribute it every Monday morning.)

Ensuring that good ideas are shared

Disseminating good practice or sharing good ideas is central to improving teaching. Heads of department play a pivotal role in ensuring that good ideas are shared both within and between departments.

Providing opportunities for teachers to observe good practice

Who does the bulk of lesson observations in each department? The head of department or less experienced colleagues? Heads of department clearly need to observe members of their team teach. However, less experienced teachers can benefit enormously from seeing experienced colleagues in action. Although any peer observation programme will be heavily influenced by whole-school policy, heads of department have a role to play in giving teachers the opportunity to observe their colleagues teach. It needn't be whole lessons; covering a teacher's class for ten minutes while they watch a particular part of a lesson can sometimes be enough.

Identifying the bit to tweak

Whether the emphasis is on coaching or monitoring (page 215), heads of department must be aware of the relative strengths and weaknesses of both individual teachers and the department as a whole. Pinpointing the precise area for improvement, particularly when practice is already good, is a skilled business and heavily dependent upon the observation skills discussed in Section Four, *Leading the improvement process* (page 153). For many middle managers observing colleagues teach is a relatively new requirement and a significant challenge. Not surprisingly, many middle managers would benefit from high quality training in this area.

Providing feedback

If observing colleagues teach presents middle managers with a new and demanding challenge, it is nothing compared to that of giving feedback on teachers' performance – particularly if that feedback contains a negative element. Yet feeding back to teachers on their performance in the classroom is fundamental to helping them move forward. If the emphasis in the way feedback is given differs in a coaching compared to a monitoring situation, many of the core principles remain the same. However, whichever role middle managers are being asked to play – and often it is a bit of both – the fact that they require training in order to give truly effective feedback is beyond doubt.

Training for middle managers

The extent to which schools successfully develop and improve the quality of teaching is heavily dependent upon the quality of the middle management tier. That, and the fact that the role of the middle manager has evolved considerably in recent years, demands that schools invest in high quality, ongoing professional development programmes for these key people. Although

Effective Feedback
The golden rules

- Must happen within 24 hours of the event.

- Neutral venue – uninterrupted.

- Be clear about what you want to say.

- Give the teacher the first chance to talk. Encourage him or her to reflect upon and evaluate his or her own teaching.

- Focus on the strategies, not on the person – the teaching, not the teacher.

- Feed back factual information ('Your introduction lasted 36 minutes …')

- Base any judgements on evidence.

- Focus on the impact that the teaching had on learning.

- Be specific.

- Highlight the positive first.

- Limit negative feedback to one area for development.

- Make sure that the teacher knows precisely what they need to do next.

- Try to end with professional and personal relationship intact.

individuals will have slightly different training needs, two of the key training requirements for middle managers are:

● observation techniques

● providing effective feedback.

The key principles for effective observation were discussed on pages 149–158. The remainder of this Section is, therefore, devoted to providing feedback.

Effective feedback

The precise way in which feedback is given will be heavily influenced by circumstances, particularly whether the feedback is taking place as part of a monitoring programme or in a coaching context. However, irrespective of context, there are two constants:

1   the core purpose of giving teachers feedback on their teaching is to help them move forward

2   teachers are therefore being asked to change.

The acid test of the quality of feedback is the extent to which practice changes as a result. Can we really claim that feedback has been effective – even when it has been delivered in a reassuring way, has clearly pinpointed an area for development and has outlined precisely what the teacher needs to do to improve – if nothing changes? It is a bit like saying that the teaching was excellent but the students didn't learn anything.

The fact that people are more likely to make genuine and sustained changes to their teaching when they want to – or at least accept the need to – must underpin the way feedback is conducted. There are no guarantees, but experience would suggest that feedback is more likely to be effective when it is based on the principles outlined opposite and moves through four broad stages.

Stage one – providing reassurance

This is arguably the key phase as, if we fail to establish the necessary atmosphere of professional trust in both the process and the person giving the feedback, the chance of progressing successfully through the other phases is remote. People are on edge, however slightly, when they are receiving feedback. Not only are they on '*but* alert', they are also on mental standby to justify their actions and conjure up counter arguments in their mind whenever they hear something they disagree with.

When people are in this state, the chance of their listening objectively, never mind digesting and accepting what is being said, is just about nil. Sometimes creating an appropriate atmosphere and building an open professional relationship takes a considerable period of time. It may take many minutes in a one-off feedback (although isolated observations and feedback are rarely effective), or several sessions in the context of coaching, before the teacher feels comfortable enough to make genuine progress. It is a necessary investment because proceeding with the feedback before the teacher is ready to hear it is a total waste of time.

How much training have staff in your school had in:

- ## giving feedback

- ## receiving feedback?

Stage two – holding up the mirror

What teachers think they are doing and what they actually do are often two separate things. A key role of feedback is, therefore, to help the teacher recognize precisely what was happening in the classroom. There are two main ways of achieving this:

1   encouraging the teacher to reflect on the lesson

2   providing factual information.

Allowing the teacher to talk before you give feedback is a useful rule of thumb. Encourage the teacher to delve deep by asking reflective questions such as 'What were you particularly happy with?' or 'Did that strategy work as well as you had hoped'? Skilful questioning can help the teacher arrive at the conclusion for him- or herself and negates the need for you to give them negative feedback.

Factual information can be very powerful. When you tell a teacher that he or she began the review of the lesson only two minutes before the bell, or that of the 18 questions asked 16 were answered by Martin, no judgements are necessary. The vast majority of teachers will be able to make them for themselves! The fact that this stage is non-judgemental further develops the reassurance process that was begun during stage one.

Stage three – making judgements

There will come a point, however, when it is necessary to make a judgement. On occasions, initially at least, teachers may disagree with the judgement. However, if the process is to result in improvement, it is important that the judgement is eventually accepted, if only in part.

There are no guarantees, but we significantly increase the chances of teachers accepting the feedback when the judgements:

- are based on evidence

- focus on the impact upon learning, rather than on the way in which you would have taught the particular lesson

- are specific – add 'because' to the sentence: '*That was excellent/not particularly effective, because you …*' Teachers need to know *why* something was so effective or ineffective.

- focus on the strategies and not the person, on the teaching and not the teacher.

When giving negative feedback:

- be clear about what you want to say

- precede it with as much positive feedback as you can

- limit negative feedback to just one area for development

- do not beat around the bush or avoid eye contact – say what you need to say quietly but firmly, and avoid shuffling around or adopting defensive body language

- quickly follow it up by asking the teacher how he or she feels about it. Everyone has an emotional response to negative feedback. The best way of getting emotions out is to give people an immediate chance to talk.

How many people ever receive feedback on the way in which they give feedback?

Many people find it difficult to accept negative feedback immediately. In many situations, initial disagreement or denial is followed by a process of gradual acceptance. This process can be helped if the teacher is given some time and space to consider and reflect upon what they have just heard. This *may* mean – although there is no right answer – that the session is put on hold until the following day.

Stage four – life after feedback

The purpose of feedback is to help people move forward. They must therefore emerge from the process with a clear course of action. The way that this is given is significant and should take into account the following.

- A balance needs to be achieved. While teachers need to feel confident that the person pointing them in the right direction has a degree of expertise, they do not want to feel totally inferior. Therefore, try to arrive at the way forward together, rather than simply telling the teacher what to do.

- Avoid giving the impression that you have all the answers by replacing 'I would do this …' with phrases such as 'I've seen this work well …' (even if you mean that it was in your classroom!) or 'Some teachers use this technique …'

- Give teachers a choice. Rather than say 'You must implement strategy X', try 'Strategy Y might be useful, or we could try Z' quickly followed by 'Which do you think will work best with that group?'

- Just because teachers know what to do to improve their practice, it does not necessarily mean that they will be able to do it. The outcome of feedback may be to provide further training or an opportunity to observe a colleague implementing the particular strategy. Similarly, having identified and accepted the 'bit to tweak' teachers may still need support in the classroom before they actually get around to changing their practice.

- Life after feedback applies at a personal as well as a professional level. Ending feedback with a smile or an enquiry about a teacher's hobby or interest is an effective way of keeping relationships intact and making it more likely that subsequent feedback sessions will be effective. It needn't be a lengthy conversation – just a brief chat as you are walking back to the staffroom. Try to chat about something outside of teaching that the teacher is particularly good at. It is a subtle but extremely powerful message.

Langdon Park

Teaching and learning working party

Each faculty nominated a representative to join the teaching and learning working party. Enough staff were interested in getting involved to create three sub-committees reporting back to the teaching and learning working party.

A steering group, made up of four senior members of staff, drove the project. This group met in a timetabled weekly slot to consider recommendations from the working party, plan training, and so on.

teaching and learning working party brief

1   To plan and implement appropriate INSET and strategies for the development, review and evaluation of each phase of the four-phase lesson model.

2   To investigate the influences of *state* and *learning style* on students' learning and to make suggestions and develop strategies for the rest of the staff (this may involve action research).

3   To carry out action research in the classroom, involving students in the development, review and evaluation of The Learning Year.

4   To review and develop the school's teaching and learning policy for consultation with the whole staff.

5   To ensure that the development of active learning in the classroom is related to the Key Stage 3 strategy and to the citizenship proposals and that the school fulfils their requirements.

Section Seven
Case studies

1 Langdon Park School, Tower Hamlets

The focus:	The Learning Year

The school:
- 11–16 mixed comprehensive
- NOR 900 FTE 62
- multi-ethnic intake (39 different languages spoken)
- serves an area of high-density public housing, with high levels of unemployment
- 75 per cent of students are entitled to free school meals

The context:
A series of indicators – improved attendance and punctuality, decreased levels of exclusions and improved achievement in public examinations – are testimony to the steady and significant improvement made by the school during the last nine years.

The challenge:
To continue this improvement, by creating an ethos of high achievement. The school plan identifies key areas for development, one of which is to engage students as increasingly active players in the learning process.

Background:
Prior to the launch of The Learning Year, a number of significant developments had occurred.

- The whole staff had been involved in the production of 'criteria for effective learning'.
- A behaviour working group had been established.
- The school had become involved in Excellence in Cities, an SRB (single regeneration budget) funded project involving the appointment of 'motivator teachers' to work jointly in Langdon Park and local primary schools.
- The school had piloted the Key Stage 3 strategy (2000–2001). Progress was made with literacy and numeracy and the beginnings of a more collegiate approach to addressing the needs of the school were developed.
- A number of teachers were beginning to try out different teaching strategies in their classrooms.
- Student opinion had been canvassed – they were asked what strategies helped them learn, ways in which marking of work could be made more helpful to them, and so on.
- A teaching and learning working party was established (page 226 opposite) and launched to correspond with the beginning of The Learning Year.

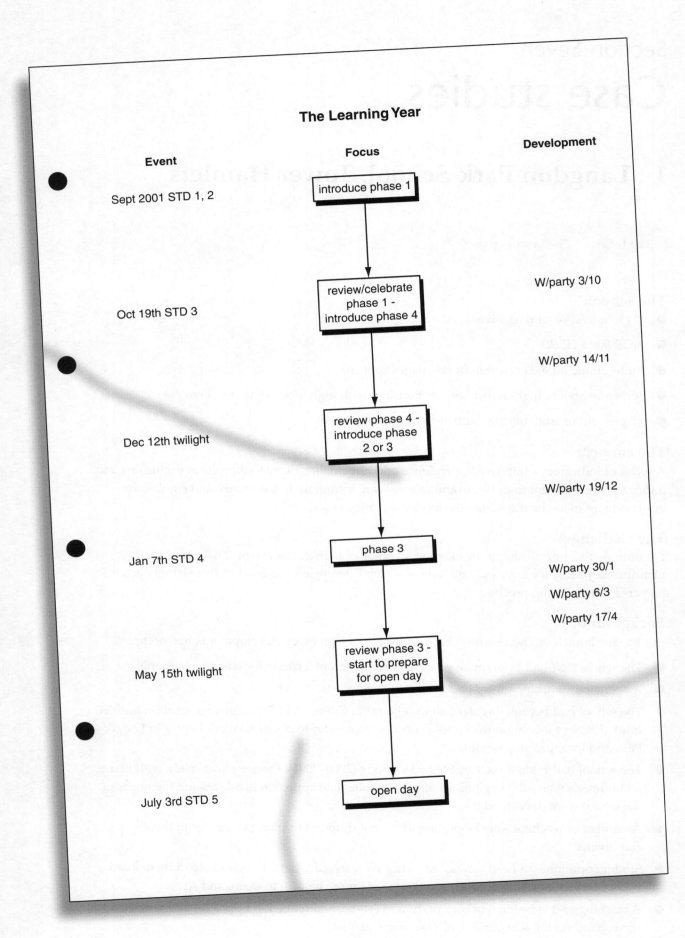

The Learning Year

Event	Focus	Development

Sept 2001 STD 1, 2 — introduce phase 1

Oct 19th STD 3 — review/celebrate phase 1 - introduce phase 4 — W/party 3/10

— W/party 14/11

Dec 12th twilight — review phase 4 - introduce phase 2 or 3

— W/party 19/12

Jan 7th STD 4 — phase 3 — W/party 30/1

— W/party 6/3

— W/party 17/4

May 15th twilight — review phase 3 - start to prepare for open day

July 3rd STD 5 — open day

- There had been a whole-staff INSET day on teaching and learning. The day focused upon state, style and structure (Section Three, *What do we know about learning?*) and emphasized the need for teachers to tweak, rather than transform, their teaching. Central to the training was the four-phase lesson model (pages 91–117).

The Learning Year

Aim

To provide a coherent framework for ongoing professional development by focusing firmly upon teaching and learning.

Outline

The four-phase lesson model (pages 91–117) was adopted to structure developments for the academic year 2001–2002. Each discrete phase of the lesson would be considered in turn and become the specific focus for all training, observation and development for a designated period of time.

A schedule was issued at the beginning of the year (page 228, opposite) so that staff knew in advance both the broad focus for each term and specific dates for INSET days, twilight sessions, implementation and evaluation of strategies. The initial focus for the year was phase one (overview), followed by phases four (review), two (input) and finally three (processing).

The Learning Year was launched by the headteacher on the first day of the autumn term. It was well received, largely because staff already felt considerable involvement in the process (page 227, 'Background'). The brief outline of the initiative, below, was provided to all staff.

What is The Learning Year?

- The main INSET focus for the year 2001–2002 is to be the development of teaching and learning in the classroom. This is to be achieved through work with the staff as a whole, and both within and across faculties.

  The Learning Year will have at its heart the development and sharing of active learning strategies between individual teachers. This will take place through our work on INSET days and through the process of lesson sharing and review throughout the year.

  While we will be exploring the related themes of learning state and style, our main focus this year will be on the structure of lessons, in particular on the development of the four-phase lesson across all faculties.

- We have used the phrase 'The Learning Year' so as to focus our minds on what we are all involved in as teachers, and to highlight this as our main priority as a school. As for the timescale, The Learning Year starts here and continues beyond 2002 and into the future.

Phase one of lessons:
How am I doing?

Faculty _____

NB This is not a formal record and there is no need to write your name.

Think of the 'average' lesson that you teach. Give yourself a mark out of ten for each of the following.

		Mark
1	Do you grab the students' attention right from the start?	
2	Do your lessons begin crisply and with pace?	
3	Do you link the learning?	
4	Do you review previous learning?	
5	Are the learning objectives shared with the students?	
6	Is the key learning point introduced quickly?	
7	Do the students know what they will be doing during the course of the lesson?	
8	Are students clear about what is expected of them?	
9	Is there a sense of curiosity, challenge and expectation?	
10	Are students encouraged to set individual goals? Are these specific?	
Total (out of 100)		

Please hand your sheet in at the start of the faculty meeting so that we can get a rough idea of where we are at as a whole staff at the start of this work. This will help us to evaluate its impact.

A number of discrete activities characterized training and development for each of the four phases:

1   pre-training – self-reflection, canvassing of student opinion

2   training/input – sharing of ideas, learning partners

3   implementation – trying out strategies in the classroom

4   evaluation – are the strategies improving learning?

These stages of development correlate with the DIIR model (diagnosis, input, implement, review) outlined on pages 149–197.

Pre-training phase

This involved both staff and students. Staff were engaged in self-reflection activities (page 230, opposite) both to get an idea of the current position and to help evaluate the impact of developments.

Student opinion was canvassed using the prompts:

● 'things that help me learn'

● 'things that make it difficult to learn, or prevent me from learning'.

While it was accepted that the results would be impressionistic – with some students taking the task more seriously than others, and some having a false or distorted impression of what is taking place in the classroom – the school took the view that it would be interesting to see how teachers were perceived and that it would be mad to simply ignore students' views.

The results were reassuring: the students generally felt that teachers had high expectations and took time to explain things, and they greatly appreciated the fact that the teachers knew how to help them when they didn't understand something.

The students' views also provided food for thought. For example, there was a consensus of opinion that while teachers provided ample opportunities to discuss things as a class, there were fewer opportunities to discuss things in small groups. Significantly, a number of students (Asian girls in particular) reported that they found it easier and helpful when they were able to talk in smaller groups.

Information from students provided the staff with another dimension to consider and debate as part of the improvement process.

The headteacher addressed each year group in an assembly to inform students that the project was taking place. He also fed back to them the results of an 'attitudinal survey' that they had completed, which was designed to give the staff a clear picture about what the students thought about their lessons. He explained to them that The Learning Year was one way in which the school was responding to their views.

The Learning Year
— draft student survey

	True of nearly all teachers	True of most teachers	True of some teachers	True of only a few teachers
Teachers:				
set us aims/objectives for the lesson				
link what we are to learn to previous lessons				
let us know what we will be doing during the lesson				
go over what we should have learned in the last lesson				
grab our attention right from the start				
let us know what is expected of us				
make our lessons interesting				
help us to problem-solve and investigate things ourselves				
enable us to discuss things in groups				
enable us to discuss things in pairs				
enable us to discuss things as a class				
know how to help us when we don't understand something				
encourage us to ask questions				
go over what we have learned, at the end of the lesson				

Training

Each phase was launched by a training event in the form of an INSET day or a twilight session. The key features of the training were as outlined below.

1 Members of staff were heavily involved in delivering training to colleagues

Middle managers played a key role in this process. For example:

MEMO

To: Heads of faculty

From: JL

CC: CN CC

Date: 8.12.01

Re: Faculty session on INSET day 7.1.02. — Modelling a phase three strategy

----

As heads of faculty, you have a vital role to play in the further development of the four-phase lesson at phase three (the learning phase). For this reason, the working party would like you to **model a phase three strategy** for the rest of your faculty during the faculty session on the INSET day of 7.1.02.

2 All staff were actively involved

At every phase, teachers were given the opportunity to question, discuss and shape the initiative. For example:

Faculty discussion on phase one

Agenda

1. What should the length of phase one be, in terms of lesson time?

2. How could this vary, according to the position of the lesson within the unit (start/middle/end), the time of day, and so on?

3. Comments on/questions about strategies suggested during training.

Phase one:

Lesson sharing sheet

Faculty _____

Learning strategy	Comments, and score out of ten
1 Did s/he grab the students' attention right from the start?	
2 Did the lesson begin crisply and with pace?	
3 Did s/he link the learning?	
4 Did s/he review previous learning?	
5 Were the learning objectives shared with the students?	
6 Was the key learning point introduced quickly?	
7 Did the students know what they would be doing during the lesson?	
8 Were students clear about what was expected of them?	
9 Was there a sense of curiosity, challenge and expectation?	
10 Were students encouraged to set individual goals?	

3 'Learning partners' were used

For example:

> # Improving phase one of our lessons
>
> ## Session five: Individual/paired work
>
> Your head of faculty will now suggest another teacher for you to work with — your learning partner (well, why not?)
>
> ### What you need to do
>
> 1 Each choose a class to focus on. (Choose classes that you teach at different times so that you will be able to share lessons later on.)
>
> 2 Working individually, think of the first lesson that you intend to teach this class this half term. Now plan phase one of the lesson using the strategies suggested. (Spend 20 minutes doing this.)
>
> 3 Discuss and develop your ideas with your learning partner (20 minutes).
>
> 4 Now think of a lesson in two or three weeks with the same class and plan which strategies you will use during phase one of that lesson (20 minutes).
>
> 5 Discuss and develop your ideas with your learning partner (20 minutes).
>
> Discuss how this process went, and what you may have learned from it, with the rest of the faculty.

Implementation and evaluation

The use of learning partners to support teachers while they tried out new techniques in the classroom, and to provide some feedback, ensured that the implementation and evaluation of the strategies were inextricably linked. Central to this was the use of the lesson sharing sheet (page 234, opposite) to generate the data necessary to assess the impact of the training upon classroom practice. A significant feature was that these sheets were completed anonymously – the evaluation focused upon teaching, not teachers.

> # Improving phase one of our lessons
>
> ## Follow-up work
>
> 1 Arrange a time with your learning partner when you can share phase one for one of your partner's lessons. (This should happen in the first three weeks of term.)
>
> 2 Complete the lesson sharing sheet. One copy should go to your learning partner and the other to your head of faculty.
>
> This is not a formal record and will be kept anonymous. It will be used to evaluate our progress as a school. For example, results could be compared against questionnaires completed at the start of the process to see if there have been any changes to practice.

Outcomes

In response to the question 'Has there been a positive or negative change in student behaviour and attitudes?'

● 34 teachers said there had been a positive change

● 3 teachers reported a negative change

● 5 teachers were unsure.

Additional comments included:

'Students seem more settled at the start of lessons.'

'Students seem more aware that their learning is the focus.'

In response to the question 'Have you found learning partners and paired working useful?'

● 36 teachers replied yes

● 5 teachers replied no

● 5 teachers were unsure.

Additional comments included:

'It would be good to do this with teachers from other faculties.'

'Common focus on teaching and learning gives us all the chance to be learners again and review our practice.'

> 'Staff development training is focused this year on teaching and learning, and the school has identified a process for revisiting this that is proving to be a source of inspiration to many teachers, by providing them with a vehicle for the reappraisal of their fundamental pedagogical beliefs.'

Extract from Section 3 HMI Inspection Report

Outcomes and evaluation

Some of the outcomes identified during the evaluation of phase one are listed below. These points are taken directly from teacher evaluation sheets.

Strategies that teachers tried and found useful:

- emphasizing the main learning point at the beginning of the lesson and stressing keywords during phase one

- encouraging one- or two-minute breaks during lessons, with students sometimes moving around

- putting questions on the board at the start to really focus students' thinking

- writing down learning aims at the start, so that the teacher is more aware of what he or she has to do to make students' learning the focus of the lesson, and the students are more aware of what is expected from them.

Impact of strategies used in phase one:

- students settle down better because of a more concentrated focus

- teachers are trying to be more adventurous – students are responding well

- objectives are clearer and more explicit

- having additional whiteboards has helped – 'All faculties should have them'

- starts of lessons are now smoother – this has improved the middles of lessons

- recap has improved – teachers 'link the lesson' more effectively.

The future

Throughout the year, the staff at Langdon Park School made video recordings of lessons across the curriculum, created a learning website and researched student opinion. The intention was to work towards an Open Day for parents, families and the Year 5 students from Langdon Park's partner primary schools, at which a programme of lessons would be run for them to observe or, if they wished, to participate in.

At the time of writing, the staff are aware that there is much left to do but there is a will at the school to do it. They recognize the danger of trying to move too fast without providing adequate time for reflection. The steering group has the responsibility and time to judge and manage this.

The staff do not yet know what the long-term results of their initiative will be, but they perceive a change in attitude and understanding. Informal student comment is encouraging, as some are beginning to use the language of the four-phase lesson:

- 'We seem to know these days what we're supposed to be doing and why.'

- 'I like this bit (phase four) because if I've missed anything or couldn't understand it, it might come up here so that I can ask without feeling like an idiot.'

The staff know that they have to deliver a largely prescribed curriculum but they feel that if they can make the learning more effective and enjoyable then the gains should be both quantitative and qualitative.

A recent Section 3 HMI inspection reported that:

- Barnwell School is making good progress in raising the students' attainment

- the students were very well behaved around the school

- the students came to lessons prepared to learn

- the school is a happy and caring community where people feel valued

- the school is highly self-evaluative.

(HMI also reported back to the headteacher that the students were 'delightful'!)

None of these remarks were easily obtained, and the school is very pleased to have such comments written about its community.

2   Barnwell School, Hertfordshire

The focus: In-house training and the sharing of good practice

The school:

- 11–18 mixed comprehensive

- NOR 860 FTE 60

- serves an urban community in Stevenage

- students recruited mainly from local primary schools

The context:

- School faced falling rolls, reduced popularity and depressed exam results as little as six years ago.

- In 2000, 24 per cent of students achieved five GCSEs at grades A*–C, placing the school in Schools Facing Challenging Circumstances.

- The school has made significant progress during the last six years:

  1   oversubscribed for last six years – NOR grown from 615 to 860

  2   oversubscribed by 26 per cent for 2002 – NOR will reach 900 within two years

  3   GCSE results in 2002 improved from 24 per cent to 30 per cent 5 A*–C; average points score rose from 29 to 38

  4   targets for future years anticipate continued improvement.

- There is significant community involvement – local area is currently subject of single regeneration budget (SRB) central government funding.

- The school enjoys active involvement of the governing body and full support of parents.

- The school has achieved a number of awards in recent years:

  1   Investors in People (twice)

  2   Sportsmark (twice)

  3   Artsmark.

- The school has contributed to a successful National Lottery bid for a £1.5 million community leisure centre that opened on its site in May 2002.

Current position:

- The school has worked hard and is justifiably proud of the significant progress that has been made in recent years.

- It also, however, recognizes the need to continue the improvement process.

- Underpinning the drive for further improvement are three key strands:

  1   the active involvement of students in the decision-making process

  2   the provision of high quality in-house training

  3   the effective dissemination of good practice.

Teaching and learning forum — presentation topics

- conflict resolution
- managing challenging behaviour — feedback from 'Bill Rogers' course
- summer school — gifted and talented review
- summer school — literacy review
- advanced organizers — Chris Dickinson course
- circle time
- steps to solutions
- target-setting with individual students
- takeaway tips for tired teachers
- study skills
- revision skills
- group-work
- memory mapping
- Brain Gym®
- NQT conference feedback
- improving performance
- role play
- storyboards
- coursework planning

The research and development group is currently focusing on the area of 'formative assessment' under the following four headings:

(1) distance marking

(2) questioning techniques and 'wait' time

(3) self- and peer-assessment

(4) sharing clear, unambiguous learning intentions that are linked to the other three assessment techniques.

Commitment to improvement

The school's statement of intent is:

The learning of all students is given equal priority.

Underpinning this philosophy of the school is the commitment to improvements in three target areas (ACE):

● **A** – ensuring that students **A**chieve their potential

● **C** – ensuring a strong **C**ommitment to the community

● **E** – providing a good **E**nvironment in which to work and learn.

Many of the very good features of the school are most apparent within the classroom. The focus on learning is well embedded throughout the school, through the planning processes, the high quality in-house training programme and the classroom practice. It is because of the school's clear agenda – with its emphasis on learning and professional development and its climate of trust – that many of the exciting and creative ideas generated by staff have become absorbed into the culture of the school.

Over the last three years the school has developed two particularly significant vehicles for the sharing of good practice, producing successful staff development activities and contributing to the development of school policy and practice:

1   teaching and learning forum

2   research and development group.

Teaching and learning forum

This forum takes place once in every half term. In addition to staff, there are governors and friends of the school from business who also attend regularly. The session comprises three presentations lasting 15 minutes each; they have music and refreshments on arrival and the room is arranged with tables in 'cabaret' style. The sessions are sharp, focused and are not allowed to overrun! The objective of the teaching and learning forum is to provide staff with an opportunity to:

● contribute to raising achievement at Barnwell School

● share ideas and examples of good teaching and learning practice

● feed back from teaching and learning training events

● make presentations to colleagues on teaching and learning issues.

The forum has enjoyed presentations from a wide cross-section of staff, including retired staff who have returned to share their expertise, and teachers from abroad who have been in the school on temporary contracts. It has been entertained by the complete range of age, experience and responsibilities of staff, from NQTs through to the headteacher, with one particularly memorable presentation given by three sixth form students following their attendance with a member of staff at an event to improve memory techniques and mapping skills!

'The teaching and learning forum is the best INSET I've ever had!'

'This is all about us doing it *to* and *for* ourselves.'

Teachers at Barnwell School

Research and development group

The aim of the research and development group is to promote a culture of learning at Barnwell School, through involving students, parents, teachers and governors in a partnership of reviewing current practices and developing a framework of learning.

The focus of the work centres on two broad aspects of learning.

1   How can we help students become more involved in the process of their learning?

2   How can we help students develop a more positive attitude to learning?

The response has been excellent, with over 25 per cent of the teaching staff committing time and energy to this research-based project. Groups of teachers have conducted research, fed back their findings and formulated proposals. Examples of the work included:

● every student completing an attitudinal questionnaire – sixth form business students collated the data as part of a coursework assignment

● teachers, support staff, governors and a sample of parents being surveyed

● students being interviewed and lessons observed.

The journey of exploration into these areas involved a large number of teachers, trialling different teaching techniques and examining students' learning styles. The impact of this process was very positive for the staff. And the benefits have been acknowledged in numerous ways – in particular, by the students whose views have been sought again in order to gauge their perceptions about the evolving climate in school.

As a result of the findings of the research, the school took a number of decisions that reflected the emphasis on learning at the centre of its work. The changes included the following.

● The Library has been renamed 'The Learning Resource Centre'.

● Homework is now called 'extended learning' and the tasks involved are more research-based.

● The homework club is now called 'The internet café'.

● Small supplementary whiteboards have been fitted in classrooms and are used by staff specifically to write the learning objectives on at the beginning of the lesson.

Outcomes

The key feature of developments at Barnwell has been the active involvement of staff in the process of improvement. It is also a major reason why these initiatives have been so positively received and have had such an impact upon classroom practice. As one teacher put it, '*This is all about us doing it to and for ourselves'.*

It is an approach that clearly promotes and celebrates an open climate between staff and fosters a culture within the school that encourages collaborative working practices, with teachers demonstrating their willingness to examine and improve their classroom practice. This is not about teachers being told how to teach but about professionals sharing tips and techniques that have proved effective within the context of the school.

It is the climate of change and the framework of development that immerses Barnwell in the process of self-evaluation as a learning-centred school. You know that they are on the right lines when a teacher claims that the teaching and learning forum is 'the best INSET I've received in my teaching career!'

'The school has the people and the systems in place to achieve GCSE results in the mid 60s – we have proven that – but if we are to achieve results in the mid 70s and beyond, then we need to look to ourselves and ask whether we have the teaching resources on our staff to do that.

The answer is an unequivocal 'yes'; however, staff need support in recognizing and nurturing this ability. As headteacher, I need to ensure that teachers have the opportunity to reflect on practice, and not just *hope* that they will do so due to their professional conscience. If the school is going to produce and support reflective practitioners, then it is going to be as a result of a *managed* process.'

Mark Davies, headteacher at Dene Magna

3   Dene Magna School, Gloucestershire

The focus: Encouraging 'reflective teachers and practice' through peer observation

The school:

- 11–16 mixed comprehensive

- NOR 750 FTE 40

- achieved Technology College status in 1999

- serves a rural community on the edge of the Forest of Dean

- catchment area, although rural, has been described by Ofsted as 'not being an advantaged area'

- mean Key Stage 2 points score on entry is below national average

- verbal reasoning quotient (VRQ) scores at entry are below Gloucestershire average

The context:

- Raw scores and value added measures consistently place Dene Magna as one of the highest performing schools in Gloucestershire.

- The school is held in extremely high regard in both the local area and within the county – generally regarded as a 'leading edge school'.

- There has been a steep slope of improvement, with the percentage of students achieving five GCSEs at grades A*–C increasing from 32 per cent in 1993 to 67.5 per cent in 2001.

- During the academic year 2000–2001 the long-standing, experienced and hugely successful headteacher left the school. He was replaced by the existing deputy who, after a spell as acting head, took up the permanent position in January 2001.

- The success of the school is firmly based upon:

  1   the hard work of the staff

  2   a clearly articulated and shared vision

  3   an emphasis on monitoring, evaluation and quality assurance

  4   high expectations and a 'can do' mentality

  5   a commitment to total quality management (TQM)

  6   a student (customer) driven approach to much of the work of the school (for example, students are involved in recruitment, quality assurance, and so on).

The challenge:

To continue to develop the school and raise achievement still further.

But how do you improve on excellence?

The new headteacher launched a consultation process, which resulted in a revised vision outlining what the school will be like in 2005 and 2010. At the heart of this vision is a clear commitment to developing best practice by *improving the ability of teachers to be 'reflective'.*

Teacher's toolbox:

1   a forum (not a meeting)

- two per half term
- 45 minutes duration
- part of directed time
- chaired by coach
- agenda driven by staff

2   professional reflection on

- how students learn (for example, preferred learning styles)
- classroom/behaviour management strategies
- lesson episodes — starts, plenaries, transitions
- skills of coaching (for example, feedback to improve performance)

3   toolbox resources

- laminated reference sheets for focused observations
- reference books and relevant literature
- videos of Dene Magna staff in action
- INSET workshops delivered by Dene Magna staff

Developing a school of reflective practitioners

Action taken since January 2001

- The headteacher shared the rationale with staff and obtained a consensus view that to reflect and to share reflections is a crucial process (and skill) for a professional. It is a process that can only benefit teachers and students at the school.

- Time – the key ingredient that all teachers seek – was provided by the school. The headteacher and governors took the view that if time was a key priority, a way must be found to provide it. The necessary time and resources amounted to the equivalent of a 0.8 FTE teacher.

- A teaching and learning coach was appointed from within the staff to facilitate the programme and provide direct assistance for colleagues.

- A programme of peer observations was introduced in September 2001. This was supported by the introduction of a regular forum for discussion and training known internally as the 'teacher's toolbox'.

The key features of the model

- Each member of staff was allocated one extra non-teaching period per fortnight.

- Each member of staff was required to observe a minimum of 14 lessons per academic year, six within their own curriculum area, four outside of their immediate curriculum area, and four of their own choosing.

- The six departmental observations could be co-ordinated by the team leader.

- A regular meeting was set up, chaired by the coach, to provide a forum for discussion and training – this was termed the 'teachers toolbox' (page 246, opposite).

- Feeding back to colleagues was voluntary but all of the staff felt that this was an important element for all parties, so extra time from INSET days was used for this purpose.

- In order to aid staff in focusing on specific areas of classroom practice and pedagogy the 'toolbox' idea was taken further and over 100 laminated sheets were made available in the staffroom, focusing on specific aspects of practice.

- A dedicated area of the staffroom was set up to facilitate staff in action research and 'toolbox' activity.

- Continuing professional development has been provided to aid and improve reflective practice, via workshops led by Dene Magna staff – that is, the teachers' own colleagues.

Teaching and learning coach

- Internal appointment

- Proven track record of excellent teaching

- Respected by colleagues

- Existing second in department (continues this role)

- Chairs/facilitates 'toolbox'

- Has three key roles:

  1 Developing collaborative learning culture

  2 Direct intervention in teaching and learning

  3 Monitoring and evaluating programme

Initial outcomes

- In the first 16 weeks of the programme's operation, 140 peer observations took place.

- Every member of staff has taken part in the process.

- To date, there has been a balance of observations made between members of the same department (59 per cent) and those of different departments (41 per cent).

- Feedback has taken place in 95 per cent of observations.

- The 'toolbox' meetings have included video excerpts of colleagues, direct professional discussion and sharing of practice.

- 'Toolbox' meetings have discussed the focuses of observations in order to try to make observations more objective.

- Initial mapping of these observations highlighted their varied nature – classroom and behaviour management was targeted heavily, followed by teaching and learning styles.

- Given that the school is successful, it is interesting to note that behaviour management features highly as an area to be targeted – is this a feature of teachers, that we tend to focus on our challenges and our difficulties rather than on what we do well?

- There has been good positive feedback on the 'toolbox' training workshops that were provided to support the observations. These were done by Dene Magna staff, and featured:

  1   motivation through ICT

  2   lesson starts and transitions

  3   preferred learning styles

  4   using student perceptions to inform teaching and learning

  5   extended use of the interactive whiteboard to enhance lessons.

- The external CPD budget expenditure has been reduced – staff are keen to look internally for opportunities for improvement and training.

- The improvement programme has provided a focus for school improvement planning – departments have been keen to draw on the reflective practitioner process and peer observations for their own future development and to concentrate even more on core purpose.

After one term of the programme, the teaching and learning coach surveyed staff to gain their initial impressions of the scheme.

Question	Response	% Respondents
Does your team feel they have gained from observations?	Yes	87%
	No	13%
What have you gained from the observations this term?	Classroom management	30%
	Improved use of ICT	25%
	Ideas from others	25%
	Reassurance	17%
	Nothing	3%

'I think that the peer observations can be seen as a many-faceted initiative. Firstly, and most importantly, they have stimulated creativity and have motivated staff through provoking thought. Secondly, the initiative both by observations and through the 'toolbox' has provided an opportunity for staff to resolve problems or challenges they are personally facing in the classroom. The third facet, which was evident in the initial stages in some staff, was a feeling and a concern that this process is another element of PMR but via the back door. It is interesting and very reassuring that within a term there has been a sea-change in attitudes from these more cynical staff. They now realize that this third facet is unfounded.

Annette Knight, teaching and learning coach at Dene Magna

Conclusion

The initiative at Dene Magna demonstrates how an individual school can implement a large-scale programme of peer observation supported by a working forum and key staff. It also shows that peer observation can be timetabled into a teacher's life without creating additional pressure and workload for teachers. At Dene Magna, the staff devised and financed a scheme in which *they* provided the resources and the time for teachers to take part in developing what is ultimately the core purpose of a school – teaching and learning.

Inevitably, when something of this magnitude is given top priority, there is an understandable worry that something else may be lost. The view at Dene Magna, however, is that nothing is more important than the quality of teaching and learning, and that the cost represents excellent value for money.

The future

- There will be many more peer observations, approaching 500 by the end of the first academic year of the scheme.

- The focus of the observations must be tightened up further so that staff are really pinpointing and identifying their own and their department's need. The more a teacher tightens up on this aspect, the more deeply he or she reflects on the complexities of the teaching and learning process.

- Increased investment must be made to enable colleagues to be more comfortable and skilful in providing feedback.

- It is an aspiration to develop and support individual teachers to be effective coaches themselves.

- The school and individual teachers will carry out a number of action research projects that will be used to drive up standards.

- The 'interdependence' philosophy of the programme will be developed, both within school and externally, by sharing and promoting what is being learned.

> 'Too often in education new initiatives take the focus of teachers away from the classroom. This major programme is aimed at enabling teachers to concentrate on improving learning – the actual thing they came into the profession for.'

Mark Davies, headteacher

Schools that have significantly improved teaching and learning are those that have successfully *created* a culture of professional reflection and have established a commitment to continuous self-improvement.

Messages from successful schools

It is not possible to identify one single recipe for improving the quality of teaching. It is, however, possible to identify some basic ingredients.

The three case study schools clearly operate in different circumstances. Indeed, in many respects the contrast between context couldn't be greater. Yet as much as their circumstances differ, all three schools demonstrate a clear commitment to improving the quality of teaching. Not because it is poor, but because they have succeeded in creating a culture of self-evaluation and continuous improvement.

While the specific strategy and vehicle for improvement may vary, the improvement process in all three schools is underpinned by common principles. It is these principles that are the basic ingredients for successfully improving and managing the quality of teaching and learning. The basic ingredients that have been used by the three schools, in different ways, include those listed below.

1 **Leadership of headteacher**

2 **Managed process**

 ● clear expectations – a requirement that teachers will implement strategies and develop their practice

 ● a clear timescale – deadlines set

 ● driven and managed by a steering group or teaching and learning coach

3 **Overall framework**

 ● coherent structure

 ● vehicle for improvement – observation programme, teaching and learning forum, four-phase lesson model

4 **Whole-staff initiative**

 ● *all* staff involved rather than individuals or small groups

 ● emphasis on teaching, not on teachers

5 **Staff ownership and involvement**

 ● teaching and learning coach appointed from within

 ● faculties nominate representatives for teaching and learning working group

 ● staff involved in planning

 ● staff involved in delivering training

 ● opportunities during training to reflect, discuss, debate, question and shape developments

6 **An element of staff choice**

 ● staff choose to attend teaching and learning group

 ● faculties nominate representative for teaching and learning group

 ● teachers choose who to observe and what to focus upon

The culture of professional reflection required for continuous self-improvement does not happen by chance – the onus is on school leaders to *create* it.

7 **Emphasis on sharing good practice**

- learning partners
- teaching and learning forum
- peer observation

8 **Draw on internal expertise**

- internal teaching and learning coach
- peer observation
- use of internally produced video
- learning partners
- teaching and learning forum

9 **High quality input**

- practical strategies suggested to staff during training
- 'toolbox' – wide range of resources, teaching tips, and so on
- teaching and learning forum – teachers sharing concrete strategies with colleagues
- middle managers modelling good practice

10 **Support available**

- teaching partners
- teaching and learning coach
- internal expertise – teachers on site for ongoing advice

11 **Time**

- set aside for discussion and planning during INSET days and twilight sessions
- additional non-contact time for peer observation

12 **Ongoing evaluation and self-reflection**

- research and development group
- self-reflection exercises built into development programme
- data generated by observation used for evaluation
- evaluation at the end of each phase of training or implementation
- clear emphasis on 'Is this making a difference?' and 'How have things changed?'
- eliciting student opinion

13 **Action research dimension**

- research and development group
- internal evaluation of impact of developments
- seeking opinion of students

14 **Involvement of wide range of people**

- students involved in the process
- former teachers returning to lead sessions at teaching and learning forum
- active involvement of governors and members of the community

15 **Culture of professional reflection and continuous self-improvement**

Twenty good ideas

1   Make learning your *sole* priority for a designated period of time. You are more likely to make progress when you focus exclusively on one issue even for a short period of time – a day, a week, a term – than trying to address a number of issues over an extended period.

2   Generate a shared understanding of the word 'learning'. What implications are there for the way in which you teach?

3   Give a senior member of staff responsibility for improving the quality of teaching in the school. Make it that person's *sole* responsibility. If it is not possible to make it the *sole* responsibility, at least free him or her up as much as possible by reducing deadline-driven, task-based responsibilities (page 129).

4   Adopt a framework for improving teaching and learning (for example, the four-phase lesson and/or the DIIR model).

5   Use a common template (such as the four-phase lesson) as a basis for planning, teaching, observation and development. Design a planning and/or observation pro-forma based on the four phases. Incorporate the four-phase template in your staff planners.

6   Define excellence. Make sure all teachers know what they are aiming for in each phase of the lesson. Generate these 'indicators of excellence' collaboratively (page 138).

7   Ban meetings – or least re-focus them. Use the prompt, 'This meeting will improve the quality of learning because …' If you cannot answer that, you cannot hold the meeting. Spend time generating and sharing good ideas for the classroom.

8   Keep the focus on good ideas. Share good ideas *between* as well as *within* subject areas. Include good ideas on the back of your weekly bulletin. Include a good idea slot on every agenda. Include good ideas for various parts of your lessons in the form of a staff handbook.

9   Make training sessions *specific*. Improving teaching and learning is often too broad to be effective. Devote training sessions to *aspects* of teaching and learning: reviewing lessons, memory strategies, activities for kinesthetic learners, positive language, and so on.

10   Set aside time after a training session for teachers to reflect upon and act on the training. For example, take INSET days in pairs – one day for input with a follow-up day for writing material, preparing activities, and so on.

11   Coaching can be more effective than whole-staff INSET. Working intensively with individuals or small groups is more likely to change practice than one-off events with large groups.

12   Depersonalize the issue. Focus upon teaching and not teachers, strategies rather than people. 'That strategy that we identified wasn't as effective as we hoped' is a very different message from 'You taught a lousy lesson'.

13   Insist that all teachers teach a few lessons outside of their curriculum area.

14   Attach a non-specialist to departments during planning meetings. If a non-specialist finds it hard to understand something, it is highly likely that some students would.

15   Provide observation training for key staff (for example, middle managers). Use videos to discuss the quality of teaching, what we mean by an effective introduction, and so on. Ensure that observation checklists include *observable indicators* (page 153).

16   Co-observe lessons with middle managers. Share your views, judgements and evaluations before feeding back to the teacher concerned. (You are unlikely to get very far if your middle managers are consistently over-estimating the quality of teaching in their departments.) Co-observe lessons with less experienced members of staff. Discuss the lesson with them afterwards. Consider how they might develop their teaching as a result.

17   Provide feedback training – giving and receiving.

18   We cannot *make* people change, but we can *influence* them. Brainstorm the ways in which you, as a senior team, can influence staff. Although we are looking to improve teaching throughout the school, we are dealing with individuals. Consider what motivates individuals (particularly key, influential members of staff) before you try to influence them.

19   Give teachers regular opportunities to observe good practice. Be specific. All schools have excellent teachers. More specifically, all schools have teachers who are excellent at *specific aspects* of classroom practice (questioning techniques, beginning the lesson, teaching kinesthetic learners, and so on).

20   Be specific. Tweaking is more realistic than transforming. Go slowly! ('Start Small, Think Big'). When one teacher tries out one strategy with just one group, we have made progress.

'Until one is committed, there is hesitancy.'

Goethe

Section Eight

Now tweak it

This book may have prompted you to reflect on the way in which you currently manage the quality of teaching in your school. It may have helped you to identify aspects of your approach that would benefit from a tweak; it may even have provided concrete examples of how that tweak could be made.

But it hasn't tweaked anything. Only you can do that. On page 122 you were invited to consider how effectively you manage the quality of teaching in your school and award yourself a mark out of ten. You will remain at that level – even though you have read the book – until you find something to do differently.

Section Two, *What do we know about change?*, suggested that change is difficult. Even when people want to change, they often don't. It applies equally to teachers, middle managers and senior school leaders.

So what do you do now? There are no guarantees, but it is more likely that you will make the change you desire when you address the three questions below.

> 1   **What specifically are you going to do differently as a result of reading this book?**
>
> 2   **What are you going to do first? (The first step is the most significant.)**
>
> 3   **When are you going to do it?**

The chances are further increased when you:

1   write the answers down

2   say them aloud

3   tell someone else

4   answer question 3 with the word 'Now'!

References and recommended reading

By Mike Hughes

Lessons are for Learning, Mike Hughes (Network Educational Press, 1997)

Closing the Learning Gap, Mike Hughes (Network Educational Press, 1999)

Strategies for Closing the Learning Gap, Mike Hughes with Andy Vass (Network Educational Press, 2001)

Managing change and school improvement

First Things First, Stephen R. Covey, Roger A. Merrill, Rebecca R. Merrill (Simon and Schuster, 1994)

Seven Habits of Highly Effective People, Stephen R. Covey (Simon and Schuster, 1989)

Teach your child how to think, Edward de Bono (Viking, 1992)

Change Forces, Michael Fullan (Falmer Press, 1993)

The Challenge of School Change, Michael Fullan (Skylight Professional Development, 1997)

Beyond Certainty, Charles Handy (Harvard Business School Press, 1996)

The Empty Raincoat, Charles Handy (Hutchinson, 1994)

The Motivation to Work, F. Herzberg (New York, 1959)

'Improving In-Service Training: The Message of Research', B. Joyce and B. Showers in *Educational Leadership*, February 1980

Schools Must Speak for Themselves, John MacBeath (Routledge, 1999)

Effective Teaching: Evidence and Practice, Daniel Muijs and David Reynolds (Paul Chapman Publishing, 2001)

Smart Schools, David Perkins (The Free Press, 1992)

A Passion for Excellence, Tom Peters and Nancy Austin (HarperCollins, 1985)

The fifth discipline, Peter Senge (Random House, 1996)

Leading the Learning School, Colin Weatherley (Network Educational Press, 2000)

Leadership and Professional Development in Schools, John West-Burnham and Fergus O'Sullivan (Pearson Education Limited, 1998)

Research into Teacher Effectiveness, report by Hay McBer to DfEE (June 2000)

The Annual Report of Her Majesty's Chief Inspector of Schools (HMSO)

'National Foundation for Educational Research', report in *NFER News*, Spring 2000

Ofsted Handbook for Inspecting Primary and Nursery Schools (HMSO, 1999)

Ofsted Handbook for Inspecting Secondary Schools (HMSO, 1999)

Learning

The Unfinished Revolution, John Abbot and Terry Ryan (Network Educational Press, 2000) [The 21st Century Learning Initiative can be found at: 21learn.org]

Effective Learning in Schools, Christopher Bowring-Carr and John West-Burnham (Pearson Professional Limited, 1997)

The Mind Map Book (revised edition), Tony and Barry Buzan (BBC Books, 2000)

Brain Gym® – Teacher's edition, Paul and Gail Dennison (Edu-Kinesthetics Inc, 1999)

The Learning Revolution (new updated British edition), Gordon Dryden and Jeanette Vos (Network Educational Press, 2001)

Frames of Mind, Howard Gardner (Fontana Press, 1983)

Intelligence Reframed, Howard Gardner (Basic Books, 1999)

The Teacher's Toolkit, Paul Ginnis (Crown House Publishing, 2002)

Emotional Intelligence, Daniel Goleman (Bloomsbury Publishing, 1996)

Righting the Educational Conveyor Belt, Michael Grinder (Metamorphous Press, 1991)

The Dominance Factor, Carla Hannaford (Great Ocean, 1997)

Confident Classroom Leadership, Peter Hook and Andy Vass (David Fulton, 2000)

Teaching with Influence, Peter Hook and Andy Vass (David Fulton, 2002)

Superteaching, Eric Jensen (Turning Point Publishing USA, 1994)

Completing the Puzzle, Eric Jensen (The Brain Store Inc, 1996)

The Emotional Brain, Joseph LeDoux (Touchstone, 1996)

How People Learn, National Research Council (National Academy Press, 2000)

Introducing NLP, Joseph O'Connor and John Seymour (Mandala, 1990)

Accelerated Learning for the 21st Century, Colin Rose and Malcolm Nicholl (Dell Publishing, 1997)

Accelerated Learning in Practice, Alistair Smith (Network Educational Press, 1998)

Thought and Language, Lev Vygotsky (MIT Press, 1973)

Mind in Society: The Development of Higher Psychological Process, Lev Vygotsky, ed. M. Cole (Harvard University Press, 1978)

Beyond Teaching and Learning, Win Wenger (Project Renaissance, 1992)

How Children Think and Learn, David Wood (Blackwell, 1988)

Index

A selection of titles from Network Educational Press

ACCELERATED LEARNING SERIES General Editor: **Alistair Smith**

Accelerated Learning: A User's Guide by Alistair Smith, Mark Lovatt and Derek Wise
Accelerated Learning in Practice by Alistair Smith
The ALPS Approach: Accelerated Learning in Primary Schools by Alistair Smith and Nicola Call
The ALPS Approach Resource Book by Alistair Smith and Nicola Call
Creating an Accelerated Learning School by Mark Lovatt and Derek Wise
Thinking for Learning by Mel Rockett and Simon Percival
Reaching out to all learners by Cheshire LEA
Bright Sparks by Alistair Smith
Move It by Alistair Smith
Coaching Solutions by Will Thomas and Alistair Smith

EFFECTIVE LEARNING AND LEADERSHIP

Effective Learning Activities by Chris Dickinson
Effective Heads of Department by Phil Jones & Nick Sparks
Lessons are for Learning by Mike Hughes
Classroom Management by Philip Waterhouse and Chris Dickinson
Raising Boys' Achievement by Jon Pickering
Closing the Learning Gap by Mike Hughes
Strategies for Closing the Learning Gap by Mike Hughes and Andy Vass
Leading the Learning School by Colin Weatherley
Transforming Teaching and Learning by Colin Weatherley, Bruce Bonney, John Kerr and Jo Morrison
Effective Teachers by Tony Swainston
Effective Teachers in Primary Schools by Tony Swainston
Effective Leadership in Schools by Tony Swainston

ABLE AND TALENTED CHILDREN COLLECTION

Effective Provision for Able & Talented Children by Barry Teare
Effective Resources for Able and Talented Children by Barry Teare
More Effective Resources for Able and Talented Children by Barry Teare
Challenging Resources for Able and Talented Children by Barry Teare
Enrichment Activities for Able and Talented Children by Barry Teare

OTHER TITLES

Discover Your Hidden Talents by Bill Lucas
Promoting Children's Well-Being in the Primary Years edited by Andrew Burrell and Jeni Riley
Help Your Child To Succeed by Bill Lucas and Alistair Smith
The Thinking Child by Nicola Call with Sally Featherstone
The Thinking Child Resource Book by Nicola Call with Sally Featherstone
But Why? Developing philosophical thinking in the classroom by Sara Stanley with Steve Bowkett
Becoming Emotionally Intelligent by Catherine Corrie
That's Science! Learning science through songs by Tim Harding
That's Maths! Learning maths through songs by Tim Harding
That's English! Learning English through songs by Tim Harding
Foundations of Literacy by Sue Palmer and Ros Bayley
With Drama in Mind: Real learning in imagined worlds by Patrice Baldwin
The Brain's Behind It by Alistair Smith
Imagine That... by Stephen Bowkett
Self-Intelligence by Stephen Bowkett
Thinking Skills & Eye Q by Oliver Caviglioli, Ian Harris and Bill Tindall
Think it–Map it! by Oliver Caviglioli and Ian Harris
Reaching out to all thinkers by Oliver Caviglioli and Ian Harris
A World of Difference by Rosemary Sage
New Tools for Learning: Accelerated learning meets ICT by John Davitt
Exciting ICT in History by Ben Walsh
Exciting ICT in Maths by Alison Clark-Jeavons
Exciting ICT in English by Tony Archdeacon

For more information and ordering details, please consult our website www.networkpress.co.uk